HOOKER'S THEOLOGY OF COMMON PRAYER

THE FIFTH BOOK OF THE POLITY PARAPHRASED AND EXPANDED INTO A COMMENTARY ON THE PRAYER BOOK

JOHN S. MARSHALL
Professor of Philosophy
The University of the South

THE UNIVERSITY PRESS
AT THE UNIVERSITY OF THE SOUTH
Sewanee, Tennessee, 1956

The preparation of the manuscript of this book was aided by funds
from the Faculty Research Grants of The University of the South

PREFACE

FOR the churchman the most significant book of the *Ecclesiastical Polity* is the fifth, for it is in this book that Hooker defends the Prayer Book, its polity, sacraments and general worship. Yet this same fifth book is disappointing because it is incoherent and disorganized, and is like a series of sermons in which the preacher defends the Prayer Book against the many attacks of the Puritans. It is difficult to discover a general pattern of positive argument in it and to lay bare Hooker's fundamental conception of public worship.

There have been many attempts to make the fifth book useable, for it contains a defense of the Prayer Book. It exhibits our Common Prayer as a worship in the tradition of the Catholic faith and yet reformed and restored by reference to biblical and patristic standards. Yet all attempts to make the theology of the fifth book clear and explicit have failed because they have reflected the incoherence of the book itself.

What is needed is a study of the backgrounds of Hooker's philosophy and theology, because, more than we realize, Hooker used contemporary scholastic philosophers and theologians as his guide. He knew and admired Bellarmine, de Soto and Cajetanus. However, he is not an uncritical unreformed Western Churchman, for he most certainly accepts the authority of the Anglican Book of Common Prayer. Still he appreciates the Catholic faith presented to us in the Prayer Book, and he accepts as the general framework of his system the scheme of thought of the contemporary schoolmen of the continent. That means that he is an Aristotelian, and an Aristotelian who accepts the general tradition of the School of Aquinas.

However, Hooker's Aristotelianism is reformed and modernized, for in the strictest sense he is not a scholastic. There were Anglican scholastics,—Griffith Powell, Matthew Gwinne, and later the Aberdeen Doctors; but Hooker was not one of them. He rejected the subtleties of the scholastic dialectic and the intricacies of their metaphysics. Nevertheless, he did use the tradition of the schools and laid bare the inner meaning of the great tradition of Christian Aristotelianism. Hooker saves scholasticism from itself, and exhibits its inner meaning. He reveals its abiding significance as a philosophy and theology of God as a God of law and order, the one who has created the world and now preserves it by his providential care. The world which he has created is a world of law and order. Man is free, but has sinned and has brought about such disorder that he no longer finds the fulness of his life in that unique source of all his joy, God himself. Man's salvation, therefore, demands the restoration of communion between man and God, and this has been reestablished through the mediatorship of Jesus Christ. The grace of the mediatorship of Christ is made available to us through the sacraments. Here is the heart of Thomism. The very essence of the tradition of St. Thomas is asserted and expounded by Hooker; and by its aid he opposes the irrationalism of Puritanism.

Hooker is a reformed Aristotelian schoolman, just as he is a reformed Catholic. The outlines of Hooker's theology are, therefore, not unlike those of such a scholastic of our day as Garrigou-Lagrange. Both the Anglican theologian of the reign of Elizabeth and the Roman theologian of our day have drawn from the same sources. However, Hooker and Garrigou-Lagrange only agree in outline; in detail they disagree. The complexity in which the Roman schoolman delights has disappeared in Hooker, and in its place has appeared a biblical and patristic simplicity. Hooker is in the tradition of the schools, but he reforms that tradition and makes it into a new scheme with a biblical beauty all its own.

In preparing the present book in which Hooker's conception of common worship is presented, I have learned the outlines of the argument from the schoolmen of Hooker's day. That is what he presupposed and that is what I had to supply. The details of the reformed biblical, patristic Anglican synthesis Hooker supplies himself; they are all there in the words of the fifth book. I have fitted these details into the framework of the general system of Thomistic philosophy and theology.

Hooker has one of the characteristics of every great philosophical and theological genius: he is able to synthesize. What we have in the *Polity* is a new synthesis, an Anglican synthesis of school divinity with biblical and patristic divinity. The result is a theology of the Book of Common Prayer. Hooker is *par excellence* the theologian of the Prayer Book; he creates a theology of public worship as the means of giving human life its true completion through communion with God. He reveals a theology of public prayer which gives a new orientation to Christian Aristotelian theology and makes the theology of the Prayer Book in many respects like that of the Christian East. Part of Hooker's genius is his use of the Greek Fathers, and this makes it possible for him to exhibit worship as a corporate act.

Hooker anticipates much in modern theological development, and so his theology, although written yesterday, sounds as if it were written today. He speaks as does Congar of the mutual relations of reformation and tradition. He speaks as does Danielou of the mystical corporate life of the Church. He speaks as does Garrigou-Lagrange of our participation in Christ the Mediator. He speaks as does Nygren of predestination and justification. He speaks as does Temple of the Eucharist as an instrument of God's grace. Woven into a work of ancient controversy is a positive theology suited as much to our day as to the age of Elizabeth the first.

Since Hooker writes much more like an ancient than like a contemporary author, it is quite appropriate that in the amplification and paraphrasing of the Fifth Book of the *Polity*, I should employ a method so successfully used by Professor Lane Cooper in making Aristotle's *Poetics* useful to the modern student of literature. Professor Cooper has even given us a reconstruction of Aristotle's conception of comedy by using hints from the Greek commentary material in conjunction with Aristotle's own writings. Professor Cooper's *Aristotle On the Art of Poetry* and his *An Aristotelian Theory of Comedy* have given me the clue to my reconstruction and interpretation of Hooker. I have combined the methods of Professor Cooper's two books. I have reconstructed from Hooker by the aid of contemporary writers the structure of the argument, and then I have amplified and paraphrased Hooker himself. Like Professor Cooper I have at times used recent illustrative material.

To make the work of greater use to the modern reader I have used the Authorized version of 1611 for biblical quotation instead of the Geneva version employed by Hooker; and since this is a commentary on the *Book of Common Prayer*, I have quoted the Psalms in the Prayer Book version. As I have not wished to correct Hooker's interpretation of the Fathers, I have simply paraphrased his translations of patristic material into modern English.

I have presented this theology of the Prayer Book, not as a learned treatise of foot notes and elaborate reconstruction. Rather, I have used the outlines of the argument implied, and have rewoven the tapestry of Hooker's thought. Often I have paraphrased his own words; at other times I have myself written the argument, using the details furnished by him. Hooker's conception is so able, his design is so magnificent, I only hope that I have been able to make his theology manifest to churchmen who desire to know the theology of their Prayer Book as conceived by the greatest of Anglican theologians.

JOHN S. MARSHALL

Quinquagesima, 1956

CONTENTS

PART ONE

THE SUBSTANCE OF RELIGION

PART TWO

RELIGION AND PUBLIC WORSHIP

PART THREE

THE INSTRUMENTS OF PUBLIC WORSHIP

PART FOUR

THE MINISTERS OF PUBLIC WORSHIP

PART FIVE

THE SIGNIFICANCE OF PUBLIC PRAYER

PART SIX

THE VIRTUE OF THE SACRAMENTS

PART SEVEN

BAPTISM AND THE EUCHARIST

I. THE SUBSTANCE OF RELIGION

CHAPTER I

The Ultimate Goal of Human Life

THE goal of our striving is the ultimate end of our lives. It is the eternal fruition of all good. It is the highest good, the *summum bonum;* it is the supreme good of complete felicity. All men desire it, and no one in his heart of hearts really despises it. The most desperate man, the man who thinks he despises God and all that pertains to him, the man who hates godly living,—even he ardently wishes for happiness. The difference between the righteous man and the one who is perverse and wanders from righteousness does not consist in the fact that the righteous man wants happiness and the perverse man does not. Both desire it, and so their difference does not lie in that desire. It lies in the road each follows, and the means each uses to gain the ultimate goal.

There is a subordination of one good to another in life, and all of these goods should lead to our eternal happiness. Food, clothes, honor, wealth, pleasure are all good things. They are, however, really only means to happiness. As they are only means, or steps, on the road to happiness, their value lies in their contribution to that happiness. Every man desires food and clothes because these are necessary goods for life. Our Lord is not condemning food and clothes when he tells us, "Take no thought for your life, what ye shall eat, or what ye shall drink; nor yet for your body, what ye shall put on. Is not the life more than meat, and the body more than raiment?"[1] What he is condemning is the pursuit of food and clothes as the ultimate end of life; for life is more than meat, and the body is more than raiment. The mistake lies not in the desiring of food and clothes, but in the reason for which they are desired. These

[1] Mt. 6. 25.

should be subordinate to the higher good of life; they should not become the ultimate goal of our endeavor. Our real treasure is a higher goal, and food, clothes, honor and wealth are only means to a higher joy and felicity. If we make these lower goods the end of life we are led astray, and miss the road which leads to our highest felicity.

Our highest good consists in such a perfection of life as leaves us nothing more to desire. It is found in happiness. With that our souls are satisfied, and with that they are content; they rejoice and thirst no more. But some of the things we desire are not wished for on account of themselves, and are desired as instruments. Food and raiment are of this sort. Other things are desired for themselves, but are not the ultimate goal of our endeavor. Health and knowledge are of this sort. There is an ultimate and highest good which is desired for itself, and beyond which there is no higher object of our desire. The lower goods are necessary, for we must eat to live, and we must live in order to reach the highest goal of our endeavor. However, without the highest goal there is no final satisfaction and no highest good in life.

To make food, clothes, or even health and knowledge, the highest good is to go astray. Our ultimate good must be that which can be infinitely desired, and that can only be a being of infinite goodness. No good is infinite except God. Hence, he is our felicity and bliss. Our joy is only complete as we have fellowship with him. We are fully happy when we enjoy God as that good which satisfies our souls in every aspect of our being. God alone satisfies us with everlasting delight.

Happiness is the state in which we possess that which really satisfies us, but we are not capable of this perfection here on earth. We have too many defects of body and imperfections of mind, and the best things we do are done with effort and with constant interruptions because of our lack of constancy. Our union with God here on earth is incomplete, but in so far as we do gain a perfection of life, we do have a foretaste of that living water of goodness which, when a man drinks of it, will make him never to thirst again.[2] No creature lower than man is capable of such happiness, for the perfection of an ox or an ass consists only in a good which involves no union with God. The perfection of man, however, consists in our completion in God, and only through fellowship and union with him do we come to our perfection, our felicity and bliss.

It is now clear that there are three degrees of perfection which humans seek. The lowest degree is the life of food, clothes and physical reproduction. Its aims are sensual, and consist of those things required for the continued existence of life itself, and for its physical adornment. The second and higher degree is that of moral and civic life, that life in which moral responsibility to self and to others finds its place. It is the life of integrity and honor. It is a life of such dignity that it transcends the perfection of all beings below man; it is the perfection of the moral and civic life of man. Last of all, there is a third degree of human perfection which transcends the other two. That there is such a perfection is indicated by the nature of human desire itself, for man is not content with the preservation of his life, nor even with the life of moral and civic goodness. He craves something even beyond moral and civic perfection; he craves that which surpasses merely earthly goodness. There is a secret desire which incites us on to a perfection which is beyond the earthly, and is found only in the heavenly.

The excellencies of life, found in these three degrees are the virtues. Even the excellence of man in union with God is a virtue, the virtue of godliness or pure religion. The task of perfecting human life is the task of producing the excellencies of life, the virtues. These are not hereditary endowments, or even unconditioned gifts of God; they are achievements. We work out our salvation with fear and trembling, and only by

[2]Jn. 4. 14.

labor can the excellence of life be purchased. In this respect, the highest good is only given to us for a price.

The highest aspects of human excellence involve an achievement of the whole man,—desire, intellect and will. Even in pure religion, when we are united with God, our understanding and our will are as active as in the other virtues. In creating the excellence of human life we do not act blindly, but with freedom and with knowledge. The doing of the things we purpose is for us a matter of effort and of choice. We apprehend what we know to be a good, we choose it, and then work for the result desired because we will do it rather than to leave it undone.

We do not choose to do a thing unless the thing is within our power to do or to be left undone. If the star moves in its course, there is no choice made by the star. It follows its nature, and moves in its appointed way; but where there is choice there is the freedom of will, in which one thing is accepted in preference to another. If I will to do a thing, I deliberately bend my soul to the possession or the achieving of that which seems good to me. Men choose goodness, and they do so because they judge things to be good. Hence, reason is the eye by which we see what is good. So there are two principal sources of that human action which leads to virtue. The one source is that of insight or reason; it points out to us what is excellent or virtuous. The other source is will or choice; it bends us to that good which reason has pointed out to us.

The will functions in relation to desire, but differs greatly from desire. There must be desire if will is to choose. The task of will is to choose that desire which yearns for the higher good; but the object of desire is whatever good may be wished for. The object of will is the good which reason points out. The desires such as hunger, grief and fear are not altogether in our power; they come without our bidding. The will, however, may choose, and its dispositions are within our power. Desire solicits the will, but will controls the desire. What desire wishes, will often rejects. The only kind of desire involved in the will itself is the desire for the good itself. Therefore, the will, which is controlled by reason, can prescribe the thing to be desired.

All the excellencies of human life, including the highest, are only achieved by a constant disposition of the will; they require a perpetuity of virtue, and virtue is habitual. That does not mean that we are always exercising virtue, but it does mean that there is a perpetual or constant disposition in that direction, and that we do carry out that form of activity at appropriate times and occasions. The just man, the brave man, the liberal man, the temperate man, the godly man, are those who are just, valliant, liberal, temperate and godly whenever these types of excellence are appropriate.

We cannot exercise all the virtues at any one moment because we are conditioned by time, and many duties cannot be done at one and the same moment. There is an appropriateness about virtue. Virtue as the excellence of life means action that is wholly appropriate. Therefore, our virtues are appropriate and habitual dispositions of our character. They are a constant aspect of our persons, but not a constant mode of our activity. They are our habitual way of action when the appropriate occasion arises. They are a disposition of character which appears at appropriate times, but which does not function without intermission.

Virtue, however, only comes into full maturity through our repeated activity. The seeds of godliness sown in our heart only come into maturity by constant growth. The constancy of well-doing is never achieved unless a habit is formed. We must continue to do well if we are to have the habit of doing well. We cannot perfect ourselves in virtue except by constantly achieving virtue or excellence in the manifold acts of our life. Our tendencies need to be disciplined and guided by will in order to be perfected, but this cannot be accomplished through a single choice. When we first try to do well, these earliest attempts are crude; yet they are to be approved because they are moving toward excellence.

Our prayer should be "Preserve, Lord, these good and gracious beginnings that they suddenly dry not up like the morning dew, but may prosper and grow up as the trees which rivers of water keep always flourishing."[3] It is very foolish to despise the day of small beginnings, because virtue can only grow as our good intention becomes habitual, and an excellent way of life becomes a habit.

The most excellent perfection of any virtue is only achieved through constant choice. It is never a gift of God, bestowed upon us without effort and direction of will by us. As virtue is necessary for obtaining felicity, and felicity is the reward of virtue, felicity is never given to us, even by God, except as a reward for our efforts. "Blessed *are* they which do hunger and thirst after righteousness."[4] Blessedness or felicity requires watchfulness and prayer, and the constancy of vigilant endeavor.[5] In the Olympic Games it is not the most perfect or the strongest who win the prize, but those who enter the contest and run the course. So it is in the matter of blessedness; it is not the one who does nothing, and is simply favored by God who wins "the prize of the high calling of God."[6] Rather, it is the man who strives day by day for virtue, and whose excellence of achievement is rewarded by the precious gift of felicity.

It does not detract from the divine majesty or from the divine mercy that God asks of us to be constant in our endeavor, rather than slothful and disinterested. A medicine does not heal us if we do not take it; a food does not nourish us if we do not eat it. So felicity cannot be ours unless we reach forth and grasp it. Our God in his mercy does not drive us to the life of

[3]Hooker's prayer, composed out of several passages of Scripture.
[4]Mt. 5. 6.
[5]Mt. 26. 41.
[6]Phil. 3. 14.

blessedness, but draws us to it by the hope of obtaining it. The God of life draws us with the cords of love, and with the anticipation of the satisfaction of our deepest longing. He does not drive us with a lash or thrust us forward with a goad. As felicity is the highest satisfaction, so it is the greatest possible reward for our efforts, and if we will not seek it, God will not compel us to pursue that which we do not choose. God does give us a reward, for great is our "reward in heaven"; but it is a reward which is only for him who seeks it. "Seek, and ye shall find; knock, and it shall be opened unto you."[7]

As felicity is not given to us without constancy and effort, so virtue as the condition of felicity is not an outright gift, but only comes as a divine reward for our endeavor. God does help us; he helps us to achieve those excellencies of life which are the virtues. In the end he joins himself to us. But without our own constant vigilance and endeavor the achievement is impossible. The joy of felicity is ours when the deep inclinations of life come to fruition. God gives the reward of felicity to the man who has wrought out the excellence of life. The virtues are not handed to us by God without our efforts. Even God's own gift of himself to us only becomes our felicity when we perfectly love him.

[7]Mt. 7. 7.

CHAPTER II

The Love of God as The Ultimate Goal of Human Life

OUR hearts are restless for God, and only in him can we find our peace. God alone satisfies us because he alone answers every need of human life. A true love for God requires our heart, our soul, our strength. Only in the devotion of our whole life to God do we find ourselves in God. The love for God requires the highest of human energies. It is the complete man, completely loving God, who, in his love for God, answers God's love for him. "We love him, because he first loved us",[1] but in the fellowship of love between God and us we too must love. That is the reason why religion is the fruition of our full nature. It is the ultimate end of our lives.

God as the first cause of the universe is the source of our being. He is, however, not only the source of our existence, but the highest good as well. Because his love for us is the source of our love for him, he is literally the goal of our endeavor. He alone is our peace. God, as the infinite, is the only adequate goal for the infinitude of human desire. Despite all his waywardness, man is restless until he finds the satisfaction of his infinite thirst in the boundless sea of God's love.

As we answer God's love for us by the response of our love, our affection for him is quickened. If we love him, then we desire him; and we then crave fellowship with the One beloved. Our restless hearts yearn for the Most High; and when we come to know him we love him, and our love urges us to have fellowship with him. Then and only then are we satisfied. As we have seen, there is no fruition of life unless there is satisfaction, the satisfaction of our desires. God is our goal because we are satisfied through our love for him. When God

[1] 1 Jn. 4. 19.

loves us and we answer his love by a love of him, then there is the highest satisfaction of love. In such love all fear is cast out, and our lives have a freedom from the paralysis of evil. This satisfaction of our highest nature completes us, and leaves our lives no empty houses into which the unclean spirits "enter in, and dwell there."[2]

The love of God is not merely an affection or feeling, because affection often grows cold and disappears. That is true of all our affections, even our love. We do not love God with all our heart and soul and strength unless we seek him and assent to the dominion of our lives by his loving rule over us. There is a spontaneity in true love, but love is not complete unless it is constant; and that means the whole self is given in love.

It is only when the whole self is given in love for God that our love for him is the ultimate end of our whole life. Unless intellect directs our affections, we worship an idol instead of the true God. The true love for the true God involves a knowledge of him. Unless will directs and informs our love for God, wishes dominate our minds; and we worship a creation of our fancy instead of the one whom we should love. Our affections then become mixed with unworthy desires, and are no longer a love for the One whom we should love. The true love for the true God is a love in which knowledge and will direct our mind to God and allow no false affection to distort our love.

The love for God is the root of all righteousness. As God is the principle and source of all things, so he is also the goal or end of our lives. All things derive their being from God, and all human desires find their goal in God. He is the ultimate object of our endeavor; he is the true end of the whole of human life. All human excellencies, therefore, find their meaning in God. It is our love for God which gives ultimate meaning to our lives. It is a love which gives us meaning because it is a

[2] Lk. 11. 26.

love by us in answer to his love for us. This love for God is the source of our love for our neighbor. As we love God, and give ourselves in devotion to him, we share his life and imitate him. Then we discover him to be not only the source of our being, but the source of our virtues as well. Then we know the loving kindness of that God who knows even of the sparrow's fall. Then we know the compassion of that God who sends his rain upon the just and the unjust alike. Then we know the tenderness of that Father who awaits the prodigal's return. Then we know the loving entreaty of that Friend who stands at our door and knocks. In God is the root of all love. Only as we love him and share his love do we love our neighbor as ourself.

If we love God, therefore, with all our heart and soul and mind, we are conformed to his love. If we are conformed to his love, we love all whom he loves, and he loves all men. If we love God with our whole being, we love our neighbors as we love ourselves, and if we do not love our neighbors as ourselves, then we do not love God. "Beloved, let us love one another: for love is of God; and every one that loveth is born of God, and knoweth God. He that loveth not knoweth not God; for God is love. . . . If we love one another, God dwelleth in us, and his love is perfected in us."[3]

If we examine two of the characteristic virtues we shall see that the virtues do spring from the love of God as their source and fundamental principle. Justice is a cardinal virtue, because upon it depends the cohesion of societies and harmonious life of man living together with man. An examination of justice does reveal that it depends upon the love of man for God and the reciprocal love of God for man. As Philo says, "The lover of God and the lover of man are of the same nature."[4] The reason for this lies in the character of the love of man for God

[3] I Jn. 4. 7-8, 12.
[4] de Abraha. vol. ii. p. 30. ed. Mang.

who loves him. Our love for the true God means the sharing of life with him, and the imitation of his character and nature. That gives us a loving magnanimity and a largeness of his sympathy. The "Father which is in heaven . . . maketh his sun to rise on the evil and on the good, and sendeth rain on the just and on the unjust."[5] If we love him with all our heart and with all our soul and with all our mind, we share with him a breadth of view, and a charitable sympathy which includes neighbor and self in one scheme of affection.

The mutual interchange of kindly offices plays a most important part in social life, and is the essential element in justice. The return of kindnesses is the principle of gratitude; and the rewarding of payment according to merit or worth received is the principle of fair business and exchange. Without mutual kindness and fair play, society is undermined, its inner life weakened and freedom destroyed.

Apart from religion or the love of God, it is difficult for a man to seek the good of others when any portion of his own personal good must be sacrificed. Even though justice does not fulfill our whole duty to our neighbor, still it is a first and fundamental step towards that duty. Yet apart from the love of God, it is difficult to fulfill even that much of the second commandment; apart from religion or the love of God, it is difficult not to exploit neighbor, friend and country. If a man is animated by the spirit of personal gain and has public office, he may exploit his office for his personal gain, and through shameful abuse make the common good into the common misery.

As the second commandment is dependent upon the first and great commandment, so my proper relations to my neighbor depend upon my proper relation to God. That is why religion and justice are so clearly related, and why we may say that neither justice nor religion exists unless both of them are present. How can a man be truly just who is not motivated by religion,

[5]Mt. 5. 45.

or how can a man be truly religious who is not proved to be such by his just actions? A man can only be just when he is persuaded that the meaning of all things is to be found in that Divine Love which gives of itself freely to all things.

What is true of justice is also true of courage: it too is rooted in religion. Courage is a matter of constancy in the face of great and unexpected evils. Even men of unusual constancy face the great events of untold calamity with fear and awful anticipation; but this world is in the hands of the Divine Providence, and much of the fear in the face of the terrible comes from a lack of confidence in God. "There is no fear in love; but perfect love casteth out fear: because fear doth torment."[6] This love for God gives us the confidence and belief that we are in the hands of God and that he will help us. The love of God gives us assurance and the realization of the meaning of all things. Only in such love can we rest secure, and be truly courageous; but without a confidence in God, our hearts are possessed by fear. "Are not two sparrows sold for a farthing? and one of them shall not fall on the ground without your Father. . . . Fear ye not therefore, ye are of more value than many sparrows."[7]

Religion or the love of God is necessary for the perfection of life; and without it we do not have that motive which gives the virtues their force and their meaning. Religion gives us the meaning of justice, courage, and the true wisdom which comes from the love of God. It gives us a magnanimity or largeness of sympathy which raises us to the level of true greatness of soul. Without religion as the source of virtue, all other perfections lose their charm, because the most excellent perfection of all is lacking. So the man who is without religion lacks that beauty which blesses his whole life. He is like the man who is blind: he wanders from his course because he cannot see his way. He is like the man who is blind also because the beauty which

[6] 1 Jn. 4. 18.
[7] Mt. 10. 29, 31.

draws us on and motivates our life is hidden from him. Only with the vision which comes from the love for God in response to his love for us do we know as we are known, and do we find the meaning of life.

CHAPTER III

THE CORRUPTION OF HUMAN EXCELLENCE

OUR love for God in answer to his love for us results in the fullest development of our lives and the fullest fruition of our living. Every legitimate capacity of life is heightened by our love for God with all our heart, and with all our soul, and with all our mind. At first we turn our minds to God because of our desire and need for him. That is when we still hope that we shall find our satisfaction in him. But when we have found him, we love him; and then our affections lead us into further fellowship with him. As St. Augustine says, "The longing desire of those who thirst is changed into the sweet affection of those who taste and are replenished."[1]

Even though we crave the joy which comes from fellowship with God, we do wander away from the straight course which leads to him. There is no doubt that all of us do want to be happy. If the hope of happiness is denied us, then continued effort is impossible. However, although felicity is the deepest desire of the human heart, our perversity leads us astray, even when we know the way to the happiness we desire. Our hearts are restless until they find their peace in God, and yet we wander away from that which we most deeply desire, and deny ourselves that which we most really crave. Such is the perversity of human life, and the deep evil which is properly called sin. However, our most fundamental desire does lead us towards God, and that in itself proves that we are not totally depraved. Even so, we are far gone in our wayward inclinations, and we find it hard to remember that "strait *is* the gate, and narrow *is* the way, which leadeth into life, and few there be that find it."[2]

[1] Aug. *de Trin.* lib. c. ult.
[2] Mt. 7. 14.

This waywardness causes us to search the end by every other path except that of the gate which is straight and the way which is narrow. We are like the man who, instead of cutting the brush from the path, sits by the hour and sharpens his axe. We are like the boy who never studies, and yet is disappointed when he does not pass the course. We are like the athlete who does not train, and yet is unhappy when he does not win the race. We do the very things which are unsuited to the task of reaching the goal, and yet we know that there is no crown at the end of the course, and no honors for reaching the goal unless the conditions are met which make possible the attainment of the prize.

We reach the goal of our desires by following the path which leads to the goal; and we follow the path by guiding our lives by the way of the path. That path is the way of virtue, and we tread the path of virtue by moulding our lives in accord with the rules of virtue, and by shaping our inner inclinations in accord with that inner disposition which produces an excellence of life. Our lives are most excellent when we find their fruition in the love for God and the love for our neighbors. The excellence of our lives leads us to satisfaction. It is where "the longing desire . . . is changed into the sweet affection of those who taste and are replenished" that we find the luster of life; and such satisfaction and such luster only come when our lives are guided by the rules of excellence. Even the excellence which is the excellence of love—and that is the ultimate excellence—requires discipline and self-control. There is no perfection apart from the excellencies of life, or the virtues.

Religion is itself a virtue, that virtue which is the root of all virtues. All the virtues find their highest meaning in the fullness of love for God, and yet each of the excellencies has a perfection of its own. The love for God is the fruition of all the other virtues, and is the source of their meaning; yet each of them has a character of its own, and each of them is one of the perfections of life.

The excellence of life is the decorous, the beautiful, the useful in life; and all these are matters of the right and the fitting. A master-work of art gives us a clue to excellence or virtue, for it has an excellence which is clear and obvious, and we say of it, "you could not take away from it, or add to it without spoiling it." It is a matter of just the right amount, that amount which is not too much, and not too little. In this respect, art merely imitates the excellence of nature. Take a butterfly, for example. Every part of it is perfect and fits into the complete whole of the organism. Nature moulds the parts in such a way that even a slight addition in one place, or a subtraction from another destroys the excellence of the whole.

The need for measure and proportion in an organism is to be found in the purpose of the finite thing. To carry out his purposes, even God must restrain himself and reduce himself to measure and law. That is the reason why he has established a law for his own creative purpose. If measure and law are necessary to God, how much more is it true of the creature, for the the creature is by his very nature limited. The measure and proportion are necessary for the purpose of life. As purpose is a definite end, it requires those means which are appropriate to the end to which they lead. The appropriate always involves measure and proportion.

Not every act is suited to the attaining of every end. There are proper means and there are improper means for gaining a given result. For example, the butcher's cleaver is too large for a surgical operation, and the lance is too small for the cutting up of the ox. Each of these instruments is excellent in its way, but it is appropriate only for certain functions and not for others.

So it is with the organs of the body. A hand which is too large is not satisfactory, and a hand which is too small is not satisfactory. What is needed is a hand which is the right size for the body of which it is a part. It should be of a size suited to the things which it has to do. The same principle applies to the functions of the body. An act should be appropriate to the end which it is attempting to achieve. Wild and random blows will not cut down a large tree. Our movements must be under control for such a task. This is true of every significant act of human life, for each of them has the excellence of proportion.

In all human activity there should be an excellence of proportion, an excellence of appropriateness of means to end. Such excellence is always an excellence of balance, weight and measure. It is always a matter of the right amount, something between too much and too little. Nature gives us the clue in the beauty and proportion of the works of her hands. There is perfect adjustment between means and end, and that involves proper proportion. In the bodies and functions of trees and vines, insects and animals, is to be found a happy balance which avoids extremes. If this is true of nature, it is much more true of our moral life, because a beautiful life is like an organism of nature, something far more beautiful than any creation of a poet or painter. Virtue as an excellence of life observes the mean; and like a beautiful creation of nature, it would be spoiled if anything should be added or anything subtracted from it.

Virtue, therefore, lies between two vices, and is a choice of the *via media* between two extremes. This *via media*, we must remember, is also the way of excellence; it is the supreme glory of life. Courage and temperance are examples of excellencies of life. They are also examples of the mean, and lie between the extremes of too much and too little. A man who fears everything and never holds his own in the face of panic is a coward, and is a man of excessive fear. The man who fears nothing and dreads no disgrace is a man with too little fear. Fear has its place, and "the fear of the Lord" has rightly been declared to be "the beginning of wisdom."[3] Midway between the coward and the rash man is the man of courage. He is the man whose life

[3]Ps. III. 10.

is lived in terms of that excellence which has the beauty of proportion.

The same is true of temperance. The path of temperance is marred by excess or defect. The man who drains the cup of every bodily joy, whether that food or drink, or physical love, is a sensual man. He suffers from an excess of bodily pleasure. On the other hand, the man who eats only to sustain life, and considers all pleasure of food and drink as intrinsically evil is insensitive. Between these two extremes is the temperate man, whose life has a decorousness of appetite and of its satisfaction.

Some acts and some feelings, however, are intrinsically evil, whether practiced in excess, defect, or moderation. Such feelings are hate and envy, and such actions are murder and adultery. The inherently evil is in itself indecorous, and so we can lay down no rules of an appropriate moderation of them. Murder and adultery are intrinsically inappropriate, and the mean does not apply to them. The mean, therefore, is a rule of excellence, and has significance only as the perfecting and giving of beauty to that which can reach the true fruition of life by following it. If life is marred through excess and defect, then there appears the corruption of the excellence of life. Excess and defect mar life and distort it, but the mean gives it excellence.

CHAPTER IV

THE CORRUPTION OF RELIGION

TRUE religion is the true love of God, and such a love gives us a proper balance in life. When a man loves God, fear does not predominate, and troubled worry is controlled by devotion to a God who cares for us and who knows even when the sparrow falls.[1] There is, of course, a reasonable concern for our own life and the lives of others; but this is not a troubled fear about life and its difficulties. "Let not your heart be troubled: ye believe in God, believe also in me."[2] Fear has a place in life, for we should fear those things which destroy our higher life;[3] but it is not a part of Christian love to fear those who merely kill the body, or to be too much concerned about tomorrow's troubles. The man of true religion lets "the morrow . . . take thought for the things of itself."[4] The love of God casts out useless fear and anxious care; the greatness of the man who really loves God is to be found in that love for God which casts out all needless anxiety.

Christian patience is the fruit of this love for God. It is merely one of the virtues which flow so naturally from the root virtue of religion. Christian patience is the result of the transfiguration of life through the love of God. Patience is not the mere endurance of the many things which happen to us in life; it is not a simple resignation to the hardship of life and its various problems. Such resignation is far too passive to be characteristic of our Lord and his Apostles. Rather, patience is the control of fear through the recognition of the loving providence of God,

[1] Mt. 10. 29
[2] Jn. 14. 1.
[3] Mt. 10. 28.
[4] Mt. 6. 34.

and our love and trust in him. It is the trust of the child who knows the tender love and care of the Father in heaven to whom he confides his life.

Patience is rooted in knowledge and nurtured in affectionate trust. It is not simply the trust of Job, for his is a confidence in spite of doubt; it is the trust of our Lord in his Father, and our own confidence in the God whom we love "because he first loved us."[5] If, like Job, we say, "Though he slay me, yet will I trust in him,"[6] it is because "there is no fear in love; but perfect love casteth out fear."[7]

Patience rooted in the love for God is not an insensitivity to the dreadful in life. Our Lord prayed for deliverance from the terrible cup which was his to drink: "O my Father, if it be possible, let this cup pass from me."[8] Patience is, however, a resolute and fixed resolve in the face of all difficulties. It has its source in our love for the God whom we trust. There is, of course, always some fear in our earthly love. That is because our love is never perfect. Yet even here on earth our fear may be under control and need not destroy our courage, our trust and our loyalty. Thus, the Christian who loves his God with all his heart and with all his soul and with all his strength is not a man with a troubled heart; instead, he is the man with forbearance and trust.

The true love for the true God is the source of our love for our neighbor; and from the love of our neighbor spring all of our virtuous relations with our fellow men. The love of God is the source of our love for our neighbor because there can be no true love of a true God which does not reveal itself in the kind of justice which is characteristic of God himself. We become like the one whom we love; and so when we love God we imitate the perfection of God himself and become perfect as he is per-

[5] I Jn. 4. 19.
[6] Job 13. 15.
[7] I Jn. 4. 18.
[8] Mt. 26. 39.

fect.[9] Thus, we cannot have for him a true love which produces injustice and unkindness. He who sends his rain on the just and unjust alike is the Father whose influence on us produces in us the virtues of justice and mercy; and from such virtues all human excellence springs. Religion as the true love for the true God is the source of all righteousness.

But religion is not always sound. There are evil forms of it, which produce evil fruits; and if we recognize these evil fruits of unsound religion, we can distinguish undefiled religion from defiled. There are two types of vice characterizing religion, as there are two types of vice characterizing every other virtue. Even though religion is very complex, its true form is a virtue, and its perversions are vices. As is true of all the virtues, the perversions are those of excess and defect. The defect of religion lies in the loss of belief in God, or any interest in him. Such a religion has become so impoverished in belief and interest that it has lost its vitality as religion. When religion suffers from excess it is animated by fear and ignorant zeal. It is intense, but it is excessive in its superstition and intolerance.

The defect of religion is common enough today. It appears as a general religious sentiment, without any belief in God or trust in him; it is religious aspiration without any real trust in a real God. It is religion without God; it is a religion of moral and civic virtue, devoid of any faith in a living God. Those who defend such a religion say that religious feeling does play a part in life, because it has something to do with high morals and political decency. Hence, we must appeal to it as the safeguard of our social life.

This is the kind of religion which destroys the belief in God because it considers all such belief superstitious. It desires to destroy superstition in every form. The reformer who wishes to correct superstitious religion, in his zeal for correction, often destroys all religion. Our age suffers from this defect. We

[9] Mt. 5. 48.

pride ourselves on our open-mindedness and our freedom from all superstition. Certainly we do not suffer from that excess of religion which is found in superstition. We do, however, suffer from that defective religion which has destroyed all belief and has been reduced to atheism.

Such defective religion produces a moral defectiveness as well. Its fruits are a lack of moral standards and a cynicism about higher human values. It opens the way to the false religions of our age. It is the first step to fascism and communism. Where there is no belief in God, religion loses its vitality. When religion has lost its vitality it has little power to motivate morals and to generate the higher civic responsibilities. The result of defective religion is cynicism and immorality.

Let us now consider the excess of religion, for there are those who have this fault. Those who have excess of religion are not excessive because they have too much pure religion. They are excessive because they have an uncontrolled and undisciplined religion, a religion which is motivated by fear and ignorant zeal. As the author of the *Wisdom of Solomon* says, "Fear is nothing else but a betraying of the succours which reason offereth."[10] The superstitious man is driven by fear, and his imagination develops a dreadful imagery which is vivid beyond compare. The ignorance of the superstitious man as to the true nature of God leads him into fear; and fear creates a world of imagination which terrorizes its devotees. Only think of Hinduism with its myriads of gods and with its dreadful and fantastic art. Ancient Greece had a fearful side to her popular religion; and both Catholic and Protestant Christianity have revealed this excess. It was Aristotle who pruned away the excess of popular Greek religion. It was the Anglican Reformation which purged the western Catholic heritage of its superstitious excesses.

A special form of superstition is that of ignorant zeal. It is a source of intense persecution and of intense and misguided

[10]Wis. 17. 11.

loyalties. The Apostle Paul speaks of himself as zealous in his persecution of the Church in the days before his conversion. Ignorant zeal is not fear; but it is enthusiasm without guidance. Because it is excessive it leads to cruelty and persecution. The motive of persecution is an enthusiasm that is misguided because it is not informed by true knowledge. Here we have a special form of superstition, animated by enthusiasm rather than fear, which holds that excessive zeal in persecution is more acceptable to God than kindness and mercy. But the religion of our Lord and Saviour is not a religion of this sort. The religion of love does not persecute. Love is not an excessive zeal for its own things,[11] but a concern for others and a consideration for the needs of others.

True religion and undefiled stands as a mean in contrast to both excess and defect. It reveals itself in "the fruit of the Spirit, . . . love, joy, peace, longsuffering, gentleness, goodness, faith, meekness, temperance."[12] The source of true religion is the true love for the true God. Of such religion there cannot be too much, because of Christian love there cannot be too much. The infinite Father of all mercies demands of us the full measure of our devotion. But there can be an excess of religious feelings; that is when our feelings are not those of love, but those of fear and zeal.

When we allow fear and ignorant zeal to direct our lives, then we are cruel and unkind in the name of the Lord. This is an excess of religion. The excess of religion does not destroy it, although it does pervert it; but the defect of religion tends to destroy religion itself. When there is a defect of religion, the moral life itself is rootless, and is without strength and vitality. Such a defect of religion causes the death of religion because it deprives it of its source of strength. But whether we suffer from excess or defect, in either case there is a lack of true love

[11] I Cor. 13. 5.
[12] Gal. 5. 22, 23.

for the true God. When there is a defect there is only a vague religious sentiment; when there is an excess, true love is replaced by fear and misguided zeal. To have true religion we must love God as he is for his own sake; and we must love him without undue fear, without a troubled mind, but with a zeal according to knowledge.

II. RELIGION AND PUBLIC WORSHIP

CHAPTER V

The Public Good of the Church of Christ

OUR love for God in answer to his love for us is the root of all virtue. If we love God as the Father of all men, and if we love him as we should, we will also love our neighbor as ourself. Our lives are complete only as we so love God that we love our neighbor. We need not only God but also our neighbor, because we are social beings; and we live our lives satisfactorily as we live a common life with others. Therefore, the deeper satisfactions of life come only as self and neighbor form the twofold human object of our love and consideration.

Yet there is a relative distinction of interest between self and other. A man may be a good man simply as an individual, and yet not be good in relation to society. The reason for this is the fact that his actions are different when he acts simply as an individual man, and when he acts as a part of society. There are many men whose lives are in the highest sense commendable, if considered by themselves, and yet they are in the highest sense incapable of responsible action in any social group. Such men might be the most estimable persons imaginable, if they could only live in a desert by themselves. The reason for their social incapacity often lies in the fact that they confuse the private with the public good. If there is any matter of cooperation with the government or public worship of the Church, they feel that their private opinion and private actions are the final standard for the group. They do not distinguish that which is public from that which is private.

Yet, if the love of neighbor is not real enough to carry us into a common life with our neighbor, then our lives are incomplete.

Love has not found its fruition, and we are left as lonely individuals outside the fuller life of society. The higher life is only possible as a corporate life, and so true morality is not only individual morality but also social morality. The man who is only commendable when living by himself in the desert has realized simply one phase of morality. He loves self and the needs of self, but he does not yet know the higher values realized when we love our neighbor as ourself.

The Church is not an assembly, not a mere crowd which meets together and then dissolves. It is a corporate group which has a life of its own, a purpose which knits it into one whole. Every individual in a social whole is joined to every other individual in that whole by a sort of compact or agreement which sets forth the common purpose for which that society exists. So it is with the Church, for all its members are knit together by a common aim, an agreed purpose for which the Church exists. That purpose is in broadest terms a common loyalty to Jesus Christ as Lord and King. It is obedience to him and his commands which makes the Church into the Church. And since Jesus Christ is head of his body, the Church, the acceptance of his lordship makes the Church into a supernatural society.

The Church, however, has not only a supernatural side, she has a natural side. She is a natural society, for she shares the characteristics of other societies of men. Like her divine Lord who is both God and man, she is both supernatural and natural. In so far as her purpose is to be found in the person of her Lord who dwells as her head in the midst of her, she is supernatural. But in so far as she is a society of men conforming to the pattern of all societies, she is natural. As supernatural, she is joined to God through the sacraments, to the angels through the heavenly mysteries, and to all holy men through the common lordship of Christ. As natural, she has a system of government by human agents, she has many decisions to make through counsel and administration, and she has the determination of policies and ceremonies according to the needs and exigencies of times and places. She does have a supernatural law given her by her founder, but she must also obey the law of nature and use the wisdom of man to guide her in her practical decisions. As in some sense a natural society, she has a common or public good; and obedience to that, and cooperation with that, are necessary if the members of the Church are to promote and to continue that corporate unity which makes the Church a vital society.

The public or common good of the Church is not only supernatural, it is also natural. It involves government and the obedience of its members to that government. It involves a public worship and the cooperation of its members with that worship. It involves ecclesiastical discipline and the regulation of its members' lives by that common discipline. Without a government, a public worship, and a public discipline, the Church has not the cohesion of a society and cannot survive. In order to live, the Church must have the same characteristics of permanence as any other society, and the first requirement is a public good for which it strives. There must be a public good carried out by a uniting government.

Let us examine somewhat more carefully the general nature of the public good in all human societies, and in this way help ourselves to understand the public good of the Church. We need fellowship with others, and we need all that which fellowship gives us; and this need leads us to unite ourselves into civil and ecclesiastical societies. That is indicated by the strong inclination of an individual who has lost his connection with one group to unite himself with another. Old people find this difficult, but young people forget what they have lost, and seek a new group and new connections. They marry and become at home in a foreign land in which they were formerly strangers, or they attach themselves to a new religious group when severed from their old religions. People cleave to even a strange nation or a new religious community when they have lost their older connections.

But such fellowship is not possible in either nation or Church without government. The social life of a great group is impossible where there is no ecclesiastical or civil organization. The hordes of Hebrews leaving Egypt and seeking a new home in Palestine could not eat together, march together, or even merely travel together without a government. Moses and Aaron gave the Children of Israel law and order, and there was decreed a civil and religious government under which they were to live. The multitudes accepted that order. They were an incipient religious nation with a desire to live together; and because they wanted to have that fellowship with each other, they accepted the law as a condition of their common life together. Human beings do find the law a restraint, but they also wish to live a life of common fellowship, and they surrender the private interest for the public good in order to share in the common fellowship.

The general character of the public good for every group is specified by the general ethical laws, but the particular form is not specified. The public good should not violate the laws of morality, but beyond that the form of the public good is very fluid and diverse. There are many legitimate kinds of the public good. Here a certain creativity is revealed in the goods of human life. In the state, there is a great variety of national civilization possible, and legitimately so, if the general laws of morality are only observed. In the Church, there may be a diversity of local discipline and ceremony as long as obedience to the authority and the law of Jesus Christ is maintained.

If the public good of the group is to be a common good, then there must be government. The common purpose needs organs of expression; and these organs are necessary because the private good is not identical with the public good, and there must be a means of safeguarding and expressing the public well-being. The goodness of the individual man as mere individual does not mean that he is a good member of the social group, and so the group must mould him and bring him into conformity with itself if the public good is to be realized.

What is true of all other societies is also true of the Church. The Church has a public good, and this common good is not identical with the private good of the individual, but supplements and strengthens it. We need the Church as the completion of our lives, and if we are to have the Church, we must serve the public or common good of the Church as an ecclesiastical body. Christianity is not merely a religion of private devotion to God, and of good works done in his name. It is also a corporate life, and that corporate life is essential to it. Christianity is a religion of the public good because it is a religion of the whole life, and not merely of a life in its individual aspects. It is a religion of the public as well as the private good. To be a religion of the public good, it must express itself in terms of the corporate life of the Church, that is, of Christianity in its public aspects. In the general life of the Church we share a common love for God, and we share a communal life with others.

In the Church, there is a corporate morality which supplements and completes private morality. There is public worship which supplements and completes private worship. In this corporate morality and worship the individual finds the fuller life which supplements his private life. In the Church he finds the public worship which transcends and gives larger meaning to his private prayers. In the Church he finds the supplementation of his morals, and the power which assists him in his devotion even to the private good. In the Church is the social pressure and discipline necessary to correct and reprove erring members. The Church not only serves the public good, it also enforces and makes possible the continuous vitality of the private good of its members. Only in the public good of the Church does religion find its fuller meaning.

Some individuals neglect the common worship of the Church

for private devotions. Such men injure themselves because
they do not share the public good which they so much need.
Sometimes men will practice private philanthropy, and forget
their obligations to the corporate work of the Church. Such
men need the help of the Church to teach them about the common life in the Body of Christ, its satisfactions and its values.
Though these men are good as private individuals, they are bad
churchmen, and so have missed the fullness of the Christian life.
They need the Church in order to be saved from themselves.
"Whosoever will lose his life for my sake shall find it."[1] The
man who serves only the private good may lose even that, and
may only gain it again in the life of the Church, which is more
than his own life.

[1]Mt. 16. 25.

CHAPTER VI

THE PUBLIC GOOD AND PUBLIC WORSHIP

THE Church is the temple of God, a holy sanctuary, the house of prayer, the congregation of the people, the body of Christ, . . . and the bride of Christ. She it is who calls the people to repentance and prayer. She it is who is cleansed by the holy water of his baptism and is washed in his precious blood. She is adorned with the adornments of a bride and she is anointed with the sacred oil of his Holy Spirit. . . . The Church is heaven upon earth, and in her the God of heaven dwells and makes his habitation."[1] The Church is, therefore, both supernatural and natural. As supernatural, she is the bride of Christ, and she finds her meaning in the one whose bride she is. As natural, she is the congregation of the people, and she finds her meaning in the common life of the house of prayer.

The Church is the bride of Christ, and so must follow the commands of her supernatural Lord. The Church's prayer and praise must conform to his admonitions; the sacraments which he instituted must be administered in his name. That the Church is such is made manifest in the Book of Acts. There we are told that those who were received into the fellowship of the Apostles were baptized, and thus admitted into the public life of the Church. Then "they continued stedfastly in the apostles' doctrine and fellowship, and in breaking of bread, and in prayers."[2] Here, baptism is the sacrament of admission, the Eucharist is the sacrament of continuing life, and prayer and teaching are the means of enriching the common life of the Church.

The regularity and constancy of the fellowship of those early

[1] St. Germanos, Migne, vol. 98, p. 384.
[2] Acts 2. 41, 42.

believers gave a cohesion to their common life. Their common life was not merely a fellowship; it was an all-pervasive common purpose which gave meaning to the rest of their existence. It was a common or public good whose source was to be found in God. This common or public good found its most striking communal aspects in worship. The old Israel found its public good primarily in the Law; but the new Israel was an apostolic fellowship centered in worship. That was because the Church's loyalty was to Jesus Christ, and communion with him as her Lord was through worship. The inspiration of his presence and the common life shared with him were the true life of the Church. The key to the common or public good is found in the common or public worship of one common Lord.

The convert, by his baptism, is brought into a public community, a society which is loyal to her divine and ascended Lord. The first duty of the Church is to her divine Founder. His commands are her obligation, and his way of life is her way of life. When he ascended into the heavens, our Lord carried his humanity with him, and reigns there as Son of Man. As the Son of Man, as well as the Son of God, our Lord's presence in his Church is the source of her common life. Because he is man as well as God, he heightens, rather than destroys, the humanity of the Church.

The words of the Son of Man, as he walked upon earth, are still the commands of the Son of Man seated at the right hand of his Father. They are words from heaven, but they are words of earth, because they deal with the things of earth. They deal with the giving of the cup of cold water, with gifts of food and clothes, and with kindness to both friends and enemies. They deal with the care of the sick and the burying of the dead. They deal with oil, with water, with wine, and with bread; they deal with money and property. They deal with birth, with marriage and with death.

Natural and supernatural, therefore, join together in the public life of the Church. The common or public life is a religious life, and the religious life of the Church is a life in union with her Lord. In religion, the natural and the supernatural form one unity. The supernatural side of religion is the life of God himself, and the natural side of religion consists of men finding God and communing with him. In her common life with Christ, the Church finds God; and in her communion with God, the Church finds the source of all the virtues which make life sound and worth-while. The worship of God through Christ is the source of all private and public worship and virtue. The Christian religion is not detached from life, because it is life lived in its fullest humanity. We are not less human when we properly worship God through Jesus Christ. In that worship we are brought to the fruition of the best that lies in our human nature. The Church is, therefore, natural and human, even though her union with Christ gives her a supernatural source of her common life.

The Church, like any other society, finds that her public or common good should not be expressed in a fixed manner, but must be elaborated in many ways, depending upon the sundry situations which she has to face. There is a phase of Christianity which is eternal, but the human aspects are variable. Therefore, the common good must be adjusted as the needs of men change. Religion was made for man, and not man for religion. Of course, the divine source of our life suffers no shadow of turning. God is eternal; and because he is eternal, the religion of Jesus Christ is in one sense unchanging. But in the Church, the forms and ceremonies and the moral discipline may be legitimately modified from age to age. She must minister to each age in which she exists. Although, in one sense, she is in the world and not of the world, in another sense she is of the world. The Church's worship is a heaven on earth, but it is on earth, and in some sense must be related to all the common necessities of earth.

As the Sabbath was made for man, so worship must be made for man, and for man here on earth.

If worship must be adjusted to the changing needs of human life, then wisdom must be used in determining its changing forms. What is needed is a sense of the appropriate. The eternal gospel of Jesus Christ is significant for every age, but the eternal must be related to the temporal. The Church soon learned the need for translating her Scriptures and liturgies into the various languages of the world. God is the God of both Jew and Gentile, and the good tidings of Jesus Christ can be preached in any language. The meaning of the sacraments is valid for all peoples, and so the sacraments can be expressed in many liturgical forms. There are, therefore, Orthodox rites, Roman rites, and Anglican rites. There is not just one form of the sacraments; there are many forms. The sacraments are the moral instruments by which the divine life is given to man; and as moral instruments they should be adjusted to the varying needs of the men whom they serve.

Rigidity of temperament in matters which are of secondary importance is not wisdom but blind traditionalism. Wisdom is known by her children, and the wisdom of the Church is revealed in her ability to preserve the Christian faith whole and entire, and yet to modify her worship and discipline into forms suitable to the changing needs of the changing ages. Mere change for change's sake is dangerous. Wisdom requires that continuity with the past be preserved. Yet appropriate change is necessary. As the preface to the Book of Common Prayer says, "The particular Forms of Divine Worship, and the Rites and Ceremonies appointed to be used therein, being things in their own nature indifferent, and alterable, and so acknowledged; it is but reasonable that upon weighty and important considerations, according to the various exigency of times and occasions, such changes and alterations should be made therein, as to those that are in place of Authority should, from time to time, seem either necessary or expedient."³ Therefore, the ideal is moderation in change, "the happy mean between too much stiffness in refusing, and too much easiness in admitting variations in things once advisedly established."⁴

The wisdom which guides the Church in the adjustment of her worship to new situations should cause her to recognize that the public good must not be so rigidly conceived that it does violence to the individual. The public good of the Church is a public good, and is not a private good. Yet the common worship should not be enforced so rigidly that the proper rights of individuals are destroyed and the individual totally sacrificed to the public good. It must be admitted that what is for the public good of the Church may be a grave inconvenience to a few.

The rigid enforcement of general rules, made necessary for the public good, does injustice to a few. In such cases, the individual should not be crushed for the sake of the public good. Instead, proper adjustments should be made to render justice in the unusual case. The rigidity of rubrics should be so modified by public authority as to make justice possible in exceptional circumstances. The rigors of the ecclesiastical law should be so mitigated in unusual cases that justice is done to the individual. Even the State modifies the common law by the principles of equity; and if the Church is more rigid than the State, she only makes her laws, instituted for the public good, into instruments of injustice.

However, the exceptional case does not constitute the general rule. The public good of the Church should not be destroyed simply because adjustments must be made in exceptional cases. Rules are necessary to protect the public good, but they should not be so enforced as to produce injustice. Because we urge the well man to come to the regular services of worship as a part of his bounden duty and service, that does not mean that we should

³Preface to the *Book of Common Prayer.*
⁴*Ibid.*

urge the sick man to rise from his bed and walk to church. The public good demands that the communicant of the church worship regularly, and this demand should not be destroyed by adjustment to the needs of the sick.

As a human institution, the Church's public good has a variable side. She must adjust her public worship through the ages to changing times and changing fortunes. She must have a private communion for the sick, and private baptisms for the feeble. She must change her services from age to age. And yet there is a supernatural side to her public worship. Her Eucharist causes us to abide in Christ and he in us; and so the unchanging supernatural good is the abiding and eternal source of the public worship of the Church.

CHAPTER VII

The Corruption of Public Worship

EVERY group of men associated together within a single society forms a community because of their common purpose and because of their submission to leadership in order to achieve this common purpose. The Church is like other societies in this respect, and although it has a supernatural side, it also has a natural side; and this natural side makes it like other communities in its general characteristics. In its organization, in its tendencies to both union and revolt, in its success in carrying out its purpose, in its failures in carrying out its purpose, it is like other societies.

The clue to the social or public life of the Church is to be found in its aim, and that aim is fellowship with God. The source of that fellowship with God is divine worship. Worship is the source of all religion, because through it we are brought into communion with God, and the communion with God, or the love of God for us and our love for him, is the source of all human virtues.

In the worship of the Church we have prayer and praise which are communion with God. We have the reading of the Scriptures, in which God's words are given to us, and we have preaching, in which the meaning of the Scriptures is made clear to us. We also have the celebration of the Eucharist, in which we are made to abide in him and he in us. It is in worship, therefore, that we have the source of the common life, the public good of the Church. This public good is piety or religion. It is a public good which is supernatural because it unites man with God, and yet it is natural because it is the work of a human society with the characteristics of a human society.

4

Such religious functions performed by the household of faith are not a substitute for private prayer, for private reading of the Scriptures, or for private meditation. The public good of the Church rests on the need of man for communal action, and this communal action is a completion and fulfillment of man's private life. As the Apostle Paul tells us, Elijah, the Tishbite, told God that there were no others beside himself who worshipped the living God. God's answer to him was a reply that strengthened him, "I have reserved to myself seven thousand men, who have not bowed the knee to *the image* of Baal." The Apostle tells us about Elijah in order to make us realize that even a prophet is strengthened by the common worship and common action of the divine community.[1] It is as we pray together, read the Scriptures together, and share the sacraments together, that we have that mutual strengthening which makes the highest communion with God possible. It is only as man shares with man the fellowship with the Church that he discovers the larger meaning of religion. The Church unites in its worship men and women, young and old, rich and poor, rulers and ruled, sick and well. In this common fellowship they become servants of one another, fellow-workers in that community whose common good is the worship of Christ.

This common worship which makes possible the fullest development of religion, is the source of all virtues. The worship of the Church has as its aim that religious life which becomes the source of all that is worth-while in life. Religion is the source of all virtues, and the glory of the religion of Jesus Christ is that it reveals its own worth by the moral goodness which it creates.

When the Church is pure and her worship is pure, she becomes the source of all virtue. But the Church is not always pure, and her worship is not always undefiled. Because religion has a natural as well as a supernatural side, its human and

[1] Rm. 11. 1-5.

natural side may become diseased and perverse. Religion can suffer from excess or from defect. As excessive, it is character-ized by superstition, and dominated by fear and ignorant zeal. As defective, it is characterized by atheism or lukewarm senti-ment. Even though the worship of the Church brings the con-gregation into contact and communion with the heavenly Father, there may be such perversion that superstition appears, and the services are then marred by excess. Or again, in the fear of superstition, the critical reformer may surrender communion with God in order to avoid the dangers of that excess which is superstition. Then disbelief appears and the services are marred by defect.

The zeal of the superstitious man makes him forget all moderation and all consideration of the goodness of God. He is zealous, and in his excessive zeal he worships God without reference to the divine mercy and the divine justice. The super-stitious man fails to know the love of God because of his pre-occupation with the divine wrath.

The superstitious man shuns any moderation of his excessive zeal, and calls every reform of his excess by the name of atheism. The superstitious man fears any curtailment of the luxurious development of public worship, and discourages any reform of the abuses which often grow up in public ceremonial. For him, exorcism has its place in the worship of the Church, and he con-ceives of the sacraments as acts of magic.

Superstition is like the rank foliage of a tree which will not bear fruit because the tree has not been pruned. The foliage does show that the tree has vitality, but the vitality has passed into luxurious leaves rather than into the fruit which the tree should bear. Atheism is like the barrenness of a tree which is dying. The tree bears no fruit because it has no life from which the fruit may come. It has been killed because the pruning has been too severe.

Superstition is an evil thing and should be avoided, but it

should not be avoided at the expense of all religion. Thus, it is to be admitted that liturgical religion is at times infected with superstition, but that does not mean that liturgy should be avoided. It means that liturgy should be cleared of superstition and retained. True religion and undefiled is neither black nor white magic, it is communion with the Most High himself. It is to be found not only in private devotion, but also in public adoration and praise, and in the sacraments of God's grace.

However, superstition or excess is not the only danger which confronts public worship; a doubt which develops into atheism is just as dangerous and possibly more so. In atheism there is a denial of religion itself, and so in those who approach such doubt there is a tendency to destroy prayer and the sacraments. In place of prayer, praise, thanksgiving and the sacraments, there are expressions of aspiration for the needs of the community. Such merely humanistic devotion soon destroys public worship, because it seems repetitious and without meaning. Even where there is not an extreme form of defect, but only a mild pantheism of mere belief in some sort of nebulous divinity, there is no power in religion because worship disappears, and in its place appear words of communal exhortation and aspiration.

The reformer of superstitious practices too often removes everything in worship which has ever had any contact with superstition. The Prayer Book would go because magic uses liturgy, and so magic must be destroyed by destroying liturgical prayer. The forms must go, and then even the sacraments themselves, for they can be conceived idolatrously. "Cut down the sacred groves," they cry, "Hew down the altars of these superstitious rites. We shall be certain that we have rid ourselves of superstition when we have destroyed all the forms which may be used superstitiously."

In this process of surgery, the tree of religion may be killed. The knife of the pruner may cut so deeply into the tree that it may die. The rank foliage of superstition will be cut away but the tree is also killed. What we want is not the death of the tree, but the removal of that luxurious growth which prevents the production of fruit. The end is not the destruction of the foliage as such, for we can gain that end by simply killing the tree.

The atheist is right in his protest against superstition. That is the truth of his position. Superstition needs to be pruned away if religion is to bear the fruits of mercy and love. The foliage of rank fear and zeal is luxurious, but it is not the fruits of right-eousness and love. The scientific atheist is right in directing our attention to the evils of superstition, but he is wrong in his desire to cut away all the leaves and to leave only a few branches. He desires that all the beauty of liturgical worship be abolished, that the sacraments be removed, and all in the name of the correction of superstition.

On the other hand, the superstitious man is right when he stresses belief and the naturalness of belief. He can point to his vitality over against the sterility of the atheist. His religion is luxurious, it is rich in imagery, it is vivid and exciting. Imagination is alive and interest is exhilerating. There is no dullness and no lack of color. In his criticism of atheism, the superstitious man is correct.

However, the superstitious man has a religion like the barren fig tree with many leaves and no fruit. He is right about the atheist, but he himself is extreme. What is needed is neither the atheist nor the superstitious man, but the man of true religion. He bears fruit because the tree of his life is alive; it is a life which bears fruit and not simply many luxurious leaves.

Liturgy may be used by superstition, and the liturgical forms of religion can develop superstitiously. But the reformer in his zeal may kill the life of religion by cutting away all forms of ritual on the ground that they are superstitious. That is to kill the tree by over-pruning. We should not destroy the great liturgical heritage of the past in the name of the destruction of superstition. On the other hand, the man of zeal inclines to a luxurious liturgy, and thus prevents the growth of the fruits of the spirit. Our aim should be the fellowship of common worship expressed in a liturgy whose aspiration is communion with a God of love and sacramental grace.

CHAPTER VIII

The Appropriate and Public Worship

GOD is altogether excellent. He is not only truth and righteousness; he is beauty as well. "Out of Sion hath God appeared in perfect beauty."[1] The beauty of our God pervades his whole being, and illuminates each phase of his action. His beauty is the fittingness to be found in his nature. Each function of his life is perfect in its execution, and appropriate to his intention.

The fitting and decorous are also found in the world which God has created. Nature is God's instrument, and as his instrument it expresses the purpose which he had when he created the world. In nature God's meaning is expressed in the activity of the natural order. It is beautiful because it is fitting and has the fitness which God has given it.

The world has order and symmetry; this is its fitness for the tasks which it has to do. Although God's world does not completely express him, it does reflect some of the beauty of the divine purpose. The structure and function of living things are both suited to the work they have to do. When a spider weaves its web, or when a beaver builds its dam, there is beauty of achievement. When a deer speeds through the forest, or when a bird flies into the heavens, there is to be found a fitness of action. The appropriate characterizes all of God's creation. The universe has a grace which reveals God's purpose in making the world. Both heaven and earth express the divine beauty. From the lilies of the field to the morning stars there is beauty in the whole universe. All is fit and all is appropriate.

Although the appropriate characterizes the whole universe,

[1] Ps. 50. 2. (Prayer Book vers.)

many men do not discern this, and are misled into the false conception that the world of nature is without beauty. This is because they consider beauty something other than the appropriate, and think of it as a detached esoteric quality. They consider beauty and goodness as disembodied things, and think of them as purest and best when kept merely spiritual and untouched by the imperfections of material reality. They think that even words as they are used in poetry and magnificent prose are too material, and so we need to penetrate through the means of expression to the pure distilled beauty which transcends all embodiment.

God, to be sure, is without body and parts, and in the glory of his holiness needs no material expression of his own perfect beauty. With us the case is not the same; with us there is a need for expression because purpose is only realized through its instruments and embodiment. There is a purpose in thought, will and character which is spiritual and not physical; but it is grasped and adequately understood only through words and deeds. We ourselves grasp our own meanings best when they are expressed in the imagery of the physical world. We only achieve our purpose when we do so in word and deed. The word, the sign, the act, are not the purpose, but they embody the purpose, and without such expression men feel themselves to be deprived of the fulness of the meaning of purpose. The sign, the word, the act, are necessary because purpose is realized through action. We are not disembodied spirits, but embodied spirits, and for us the things of the spirit are only completely manifest when they become flesh. Hence, the realization of purpose is in act and deed, and that means its expression in terms of matter.

All this has a bearing on worship. The public worship of God is impossible in pure silence and without visual forms. Hence, prayer and sacrament must be embodied in visible and audible ceremonial. Public prayer and sacrament are not purely spiritual; they are the embodiment of praise, thanksgiving, and the sacraments of grace in public rite and public ceremony. The outer form of rite and sacrament expresses the meaning of the rites and the sacraments, and so is essential. If they are to realize the purpose for which they were instituted, rites and ceremonies must express that purpose. The forms must be appropriate; they must be in the best sense decorous. Otherwise they fail.

This leads us to the principle that the words said, the elements used, and acts performed should be appropriate to the meaning of the prayer, and to the inner grace of the sacrament. If we speak of the radiant and the beautiful, this should be in language and ceremony of radiance and beauty. The beauty of the divine holiness should be expressed in magnificent language.

The principle of the appropriate is true not only of language and music, but of architecture as well. A church which looks like a prison does not express the glory of the King of kings, but may express the horrors of a God of wrath. A church which looks like a building for civic assemblies may give us a sense of democratic fellowship with other men, but tells us nothing of the King of the universe. The church building should express the glory and majesty of God. The worship should reveal to us the court of heaven which welcomes the repentent sinner into the presence of "Angels and Archangels and . . . all the company of heaven." The Church in her worship should be a heaven on earth, and from her services there should be lacking not one thing which portrays for us men here on earth the meaning of God and his heavenly kingdom.

Most certainly the services of the Church should be beautiful as heaven itself is beautiful. Most certainly the services of the Church should be as free of every touch of unseemliness and ugliness. Most certainly there should be moments of high exultation and touches of rapture. Our paeons of praise should be like the praise which is sung to the glory and the honor of the Lamb which was slain.

That does not mean, however, that there can be no worship without magnificent music and ceremonial, and without superb church architecture. If poverty and persecution rob us of the more exalted forms, then we use those available, and they become in a sense appropriate under the circumstances. Although not ideal, such worship is that which is best adapted to the situation which we have to face. So a Eucharist celebrated at night by the light of a candle in a stable may be suited to those in flight and under persecution, and has its own character of nobility; yet it would not be suited to the worship of a great church during times of peace and plenty. There the appropriate is the church swept and garnished, music magnificently performed, and ceremonial carefully regulated.

There is no intrinsic advantage in poor architecture, mean vestments and inaesthetic music. The fact that in the days of persecution these may become necessary does not make them the intrinsically best ways of conducting public worship. Under unusual circumstances they are commendable, but they belong to the accidents, and are not the essence of worship. When they can be avoided they should be avoided, and a more excellent way followed.

The way of beauty is a more excellent way, for it gives us a taste of heaven and a less excellent way does not. Therefore, to use the manner of those who have no opportunity for beautiful churches, excellent music, and careful ritual, is to fail to make worship that aid to the heavenly vision which it should be. To affirm that the Eucharist is valid without vestments, and that, therefore, to use vestments is superstitious, is to forget the purpose of worship. The purpose of worship is to bring us into communion with God, and if the most excellent means of effecting this communion are not used, then mere validity is conceived legally and without reference to the purpose of worship. Worship is a means of bringing man to his God, and if that purpose is in any way marred, then the worship loses some of its meaning.

Worship should not be conceived legally, as a set of duties to be performed to get certain automatic results. That indeed is superstition. The opponents of beauty are themselves motivated with a zeal for rigidity and bare ceremonial. They make ceremonial bare in order to avoid magic and superstition. Now ceremonial may be motivated by superstition and misguided zeal. In fact, there is much ceremonial both outside of Christianity and within it. But the matter of beauty is another consideration. It is not the beauty which creates the superstition, and superstition itself does not create beauty. There is a luxuriousness which often accompanies the religion of fear. The highest beauty, however, is not the result of fear and zeal, for the highest beauty comes from the religion of love.

We do not escape from our difficulties by destroying beauty of ceremonial. Instead, we merely destroy and never fulfill. Religion needs true beauty, and she needs it in order to express the meaning of the unseen in the forms of that which is seen. To destroy the beauty of rite and ceremony impoverishes worship, and leads us away from the beauty of the holiness of God to the atheism of a barren world free from all which delights us.

We do need a religion free from fear and misguided zeal. Superstition and magic are alien to the higher forms of our Christian religion. This does not mean, however, that we should go to the other extreme and cultivate a kind of worship which is devoid of all beauty and sterile in imagination. Such sterility leads to a barrenness of religious life. Because we wish to escape from a cult of relics or a fanatical use of the sacraments does not mean that we achieve our purpose by destroying all beauty in worship. Our task is to discover the golden mean between barrenness and luxuriousness, between extreme doubt and superstitious belief.

What we seek as the golden mean in worship is the ceremonial of a religion of love; we seek a ceremonial which expresses the beauty of God in his love and mercy. Here there is neither grotesqueness nor fanatical fear, but the beauty of the love of God for us and our love for him. Perfect love casteth out fear, and our only anxiety is that of separation from him because our love is not perfect. True religion finds its most natural expression in such ceremonies and in such sacraments as express in perfect beauty the loveliness which is that of the kingdom of heaven. Such ceremonies reveal on earth the heaven which is above, and give answer to the petition, "Thy kingdom come, on earth as it is in heaven."

CHAPTER IX

THE APPROPRIATE AND ANTIQUITY

TRUE religion is the love of God with all our heart and soul and mind, and this is the deepest need of human life. But since man can only realize his highest powers in a social group, he can only mature his religious life within a religious society. Hence, as man's religion develops, it always happens that religious societies also grow for the preservation and the exercise of religion. The religious communion, founded by our Lord Jesus Christ and made up of all those who recognize him as their Saviour and Lord, is the Church.

In Christianity religion comes to its most perfect maturity, and for that reason the Church is the perfect religious society. The highest development of the religious life of each individual man is possible only in the corporate life of the Church. The fruition of the native tendency to communion with God, implanted in the life of each individual man, can only come to full expression in the corporate life of the Christian Church.

Because of her communion with God through Jesus Christ, the Church is supernatural. Her deepest life is his life, and her deepest purpose is his purpose. Because she is a human society, organized according to the principles of all human societies, the Church is natural. Her life is in this respect like that of other social groups, and she has both the strength and weakness of other social groups.

The laws of social life are not like the laws of physical objects, because these social laws have a flexibility and latitude unknown to physical law. Human existence exhibits a wide variety of physical choice, and social and political life may vary without the destruction of moral law. There are, therefore, many degrees of perfection in social and political matters; and this is re-flected, for example, in the various degrees of responsibility and liability recognized by the civil law. Morality and social good-ness are not separated from immorality and evil by sharp lines of discrimination. There is a reasonable latitude in matters of social goodness.

Because moral and political judgment is not the result of sharp definition, we say that social and political matters are not the result of theoretic insight. Theory is insight into that which is fixed and clear-cut, but in human affairs there is no such fixity and no such accuracy. Rather, the discriminations are based on a judgment of things variable; and for that reason political wisdom is an art and not a science. It is the art of choosing, among the various possibilities of human life, such a procedure as will produce the best possible results. Here, the wisdom based on experience is of far more value than any amount of theory.

Because the Church is a society, although one in communion with God, she requires practical wisdom in the guidance of her corporate life. This wisdom is necessary to guide her to the highest values, and to help her avoid the corruptions to which worship is subject. Because the Church has fellowship with God, there is a phase of her existence that remains unchanged; but her human aspects are variable, and may become perverse and evil. Hence, the art of governing the Church requires the wisdom of making her conform more and more to the life of Jesus Christ, with whom she communes. Practical wisdom is nowhere more needed than in the guidance of the Church, for without this wisdom she becomes weak and corrupt.

As wisdom is necessary in the determination of the character of worship, we must ask ourselves how much the past should guide us in the determination of the character of public cere-monial. The determination of public worship is an art; the standards of worship cannot be ascertained by merely theoretical insight. There must be wisdom which comes from experience, and that means that the past is of great value in furnishing us with standards of judgment. Because the art of worship is aesthetic and practical, it is not safe for us to swerve from the long-continued usages of the whole Church, and new ideas must be carefully tested before they are adopted. There should be change, of course, but the danger is that new ideas which sound plausible may be grounded in mere brilliance of rhetoric, rather than in the deliverances of sound experience. There are advantages in fresh vision and the novelty of invention; but we should be on our guard against any proposals which go contrary to the ancient tradition of the Church. Because of the maturity of wisdom involved in that which has been long tried, the Church is wise when she uses antiquity as her guide.

In matters of public worship, it is the appropriate which most concerns us. The eternal gospel of Jesus Christ must be expressed and embodied in a ceremonial suitable to the needs of those who worship. Therefore, we must be most careful not to destroy the ancient and well-tried liturgical forms in the name of some rationale of public worship. Frequently it is difficult for us to understand the reason why psalm and prayer, canticle and collect, occur just where they do in the traditional services. These services were not elaborated according to a theory; they grew up as an appropriate way of satisfying a felt need. Despite the fact that the reasons for the form of the service may have never been made explicit, the services may still be appropriate. The worship may be wholly satisfying, even though the reason is hidden. The test of the appropriate in public worship is that which is fitting, and so long experience is here more satisfactory than formal rules.

Even when we do not see how those of old made their way through the amazing complexities of public worship, we do know that they did so, and to follow their guidance is the part of discretion. To the objection that we do not want to tread such a tortuous path because our days are simpler and our knowledge is new, we must answer that such an objection is born of the desire for novelty and the conceit of mere innovation. Our generation is not wise enough to gain from its own experience the knowledge necessary for a rich and satisfactory life. It is the part of discernment to use the experience of the past, and our pride should not stand between us and the wisdom of the ancients.

The success of the past in the production of satisfactory forms of public worship should encourage us to use the wisdom of former ages. There has been long experimentation in matters of the appropriate, and this appropriateness should be our guide. It is not the past as such which is sacred, but its wisdom is what we need. It is the congruity and nobility, the goodness and beauty, of public worship which find expression in the ancient services of the Church. The mastery of the art of the appropriate, that delicate blend of beauty and goodness, is the gift of ancient wisdom to us of the modern Church. If a service has been used from ancient times until the present, and if it has been used very widely, the presumption of its appropriateness is very high. In such a service there is a hidden nobility united with a grace of form; and men have been convinced of its value because they have been satisfied. Such a service should be discarded only when there is some grave and obvious fault in it.

Of course, if any portion of a great historic ritual is very late, and if it is not used by the whole Church, then its claim upon us is not that of the ancient and widely used forms. Suppose, however, that a form is of the greatest antiquity, and that it is widely used even in our day,—then the claim upon us is great indeed, and unless it can be shown that it is contrary to the Scripture or clearly superstitious in meaning, it should be considered as the voice of experience, telling us what is appropriate.

This claim of antiquity does not mean that there should be no new forms of worship. On the contrary, there should be innovation in worship, but it should be tested by experience. The criterion we use for the new is that which we used for the old: it is that of the fitting and the decorous. To be sure, there must be the introduction of the new, the revision of the old, and liturgical growth. But the test of experience tells us whether the new matches the old or merely destroys it. The test of experience gives us the means of criticizing the new in the light of the old.

In the matter of public ceremony our criteria are practical and aesthetic. As we have seen, our standards are not theoretical, and so do not have the kind of perfection which is founded on theory. The perfection is not that of a machine, but that of a plant or a work of art. Slight variations will destroy the efficiency of a machine, but not that of a liturgy. The situation is exactly the same as it is in the law. The lawyers have a formula which says, "Of the minute no account as a rule is taken." This is the same sort of rule which we should appropriately use in liturgics. A slight change, or even a slight defect, is not a serious injury. In other words, we must be satisfied if the total result is satisfactory. In matters of public ceremonial we should not seek a perfection which is inappropriate, for scruples about minutiae are not appropriate, and what we should seek is a result which is generally satisfactory.

Those who have scruples about minutiae are prone to desire a perfection which cannot be realized. They will modify old and well tried services in order to perfect that which, from their point of view, has blemishes. The result is usually the destruction of the symmetry of the whole service. If they are highly ambitious, they will attempt to create a wholly new service, which will, as they think, correct all the faults of the past and produce an ideal ceremonial. The result is usually public worship of tedious length or else something without charm or beauty.

What we should seek in the services of the Church is not mechanical and theological precision. What we need is that fitness and appropriateness which satisfy. For such appropriateness and such satisfaction we must turn to the great services of the past. Experience must be our guide, and we must, therefore, have the weightiest possible reason for modifying the services which come to us from the past. The judgment of antiquity and the long-continued practice of the Church should not, therefore, be lightly esteemed.

CHAPTER X

CORRECTION AND INNOVATION IN PUBLIC WORSHIP

SINCE the Church is the guardian of the wisdom of the past, she shows her discretion when she never inadvisedly discards or changes that ceremonial which she has inherited. But the danger of innovation is not the only sort of danger. There is also that of blind adherence to the things received from the past. Some men confuse the preservation of every detail of traditional ritual with the conservation of the wisdom of the past. These men are the slaves of mere traditionalism, and are nearly as dangerous to the Church as those who would destroy the past.

Our Lord had to contend with servile traditionalism in the Synagogue; and against it he protested. The Scribes and Pharisees made the exact observance of every detail of the ceremonial as important as the carrying out of *the weightier matters of the law*. They allowed no reform of even details of discipline of worship, because they feared that with the loss of mere minutiae all would be destroyed. For them the passive acceptance of every detail of the inherited liturgy was confused with loyalty.

Blind loyalty, however, can become particularly dangerous. When there is no criticism of tradition, the life of the Church is exhausted in the performance of vain ceremonial. When such traditionalism prevails, the only way of salvation is the removal of liturgical excesses; and then the vitality of the Church can express itself in the fruits of judgment, mercy, and faith. Natural growth in itself is not enough to produce the true worship of the true God; there must also be the pruning away of excesses. "Every branch in me that beareth not fruit he taketh away: and every *branch* that beareth fruit, he purgeth it, that it may bring

forth more fruit."[1]   The pruning or reformation of the Church
is as necessary for it as growth itself.

There is a wisdom which guides and directs the Church in her
constant endeavors to reform herself.   It is fundamental in
Christianity that we recognize the necessity for reform of the
ancient received traditions.   Judaism at the time of our Lord
was a natural growth, with the wisdom of long experience; but
it lacked critical insight, and was encumbered with a fruitless
legalism.   The spirit of the Torah was forgotten in the details
of tradition.   There is no doubt as to the vitality of Judaism;
this is proved by its long survival.   Judaism was wise with the
wisdom of an elaborate legal system; but it was also a fruitless
legalism, more concerned with ceremonial and dietary regu-
lations than with justice and mercy.   It was against this excessive
development that our Lord protested.   It was against the superstitious regard for the tradition of the Elders and the disregard
for God's law that he made his complaint.   "Why do ye . . .
trangress the commandment of God by your tradition?"[2]

We can never understand why the Church separated from the
Synagogue unless we realize why our Lord protested against
those who have tithed "mint and anise and cummin, and have
omitted the weightier *matters* of the law."[3]   Our Lord's protest
explains something fundamental in Christianity.   It explains why
St. Peter abrogated the dietary laws.   It explains why St. Paul
gave up the Sabbath and circumcision.   Our Lord instituted a reformation of the Jewish ceremonial and legal system because it
had become meaningless and superstitious.

In the natural growth of liturgy there is a tendency for the
rites to become ends in themselves.   Then it is forgotten that
ceremonial, like the Sabbath, is made for man, and not man for
it.   When ceremonial becomes an end in itself, the details of

[1]Jn. 15. 2.
[2]Mt. 15. 3.
[3]Mt. 23. 23.

liturgy are intrinsically important, rather than instrumental. Then the beauty of the courts of heaven is forgotten, and the interest is directed exclusively to a luxurious rite, important for itself alone. When this happens, the efficacy of the sacrament depends exclusively upon the correct performance of a vast number of minute details. Confession and absolution depend upon the correctness of the formulae used, and the fate of the immortal soul after death rests upon the validity of the rites for the departed. The sacraments are not the mighty works of God, wrought by God himself at man's request, but the mighty acts of man, wrought by man himself at man's command.

When magic appears, superstition enters the door of the Church. Then the time has come for the cleansing of ceremonial and the restoration of it to its rightful meaning. That does not mean that we are to destroy rite and sacrament in the name of reformation. The sacraments are the mighty works of God; and he does work them for us when we call upon him. But the sacraments are God's work and not man's; and in them there should be no trace of man coercing God. In the sacraments we are dependent upon God's promises; and he performs his mighty works for us because he wishes to save us and to redeem us.

The fulfillment of our Lord's promises to us is the very opposite of magic. He has promised that when two or three are gathered together in his name, he will be in the midst of them. He has promised that he will do mighty works for men. The fulfillment of these promises is neither superstition nor magic. Baptism and the Eucharist are indeed God's work and not man's. But this is obscured when the primary stress is placed on the details of ceremonial. Then rites and sacraments become magic, and reformation is necessary to restore them to their rightful purpose.

Reformation is therefore a necessary aspect of Christian growth. The Church does need times of reform; but the pruning process must be executed with much care, lest its surgery

destroy the life of the Church. The organic continuity of tradition must be preserved if the Church is to continue to live.
There must be reformation if our religion is to remain pure and
undefiled, but reformation should bring life and not destruction.
Therefore, in the delicate surgery of reformation only the luxurious and superstitious should be removed.

Reformation and purging presuppose growth. The idea
that the Church of our day should remain exactly as the Church
was in the days of the Apostles, is in fact a denial of growth.
The Church does need to grow; she does need new features in
her administration and aesthetic expression. Of course, fundamental polity should not change, and the sacraments should remain; but new prayers are needed for new occasions and new
services for new situations. The Anglican Communion has always held to the principle that there should be change in liturgical offices as the ages pass by.

In our day there is wide experimentation in liturgical usage.
This is merely the expression of the need for liturgical growth.
The experimentation should be carried out in certain selected
seminaries, colleges and parish churches; but the experiments
should be authorized and be duly placed under the authority of
the Church. In this way the actual working value of the new
forms can be tested, mistakes corrected, and false methods
avoided. After the results are known, then the Church, through
her official councils, can decide as to the practical success of the
new forms.

The wisdom gained from the generations of those familiar
with the great liturgical forms gives the Church the criterion for
testing the new ceremonial innovations. As the new prayers are
used, they are critically tested by a clergy and laity already
familiar with the ancient and well-tried services of the Church.
This critical experience gives the Church an instinctive test for
the appropriateness of the new forms. Only through the cor-

porate experience of the Church do we learn whether the new forms are appropriate or not.

Only in the corporate experience can we learn the value of innovations. Public prayer is not private prayer, and so cannot be tested by the individual alone. The individual clergyman is not free to experiment by himself, because the public worship of the Church is not a matter of private experimentation and private judgment. The experimentation must be corporate, just because the worship is public and not private. The individual clergyman has not the authority to impose novel rites and ceremonies upon his congregation. The public worship of the Church rests on the authority of the Church, and not on that of an individual, whether clerical or lay. Even innovation in public worship must ultimately rest on the authority of a public, rather than a private act. It rests on the authority granted to certain churches and chapels to experiment.

Public experimentation becomes possible because the Church does have the right to modify the older ceremony and to add new prayers and new services. Reformation is only possible as corporate reformation; and new forms are only possible as the Church authorizes corporate experimentation. The Church allows the experimental use of new forms in order to test them. If the new forms prove to be good, they are adopted. If they prove to be inadequate, they are rejected. Such testing gives us a ceremonial close to the life of the worshipping Church.

In her testing of the new, and in her rejection of the false growths of her liturgy, the Church must conform herself to her apostolic heritage. She must not add that which is foreign to the Holy Scriptures or the Creeds. She must not destroy the validity of her apostolic ministry. All new growth must conform to the true traditions of the past. Otherwise, superstition and falsity will appear. The severity of reformation may be avoided if the new is always tested by the apostolic tradition. Then there will be growth, but growth which is sound and free from blemish.

There must, therefore, be a freedom for novelty, but the new should conform to the old. The ancient creeds and the ancient sacraments and the ancient ministry abide. From them spring new growths of liturgy and service. Any branch which does not bear the fruits of true religion must be cut away; but the new branches which bear fruit remain as enriching the productive life of the Church.

III. THE INSTRUMENTS OF PUBLIC WORSHIP

CHAPTER XI

The Root and Perfection of Public Worship

WE need God not only because he is the source of our being but because he is the perfection of our lives. We need him because our joy and our happiness find their ultimate source in him. In him we are completed, and we find our completion in communion with him. This fellowship with him takes place in worship, and worship finds its perfect forms not in private prayer but in public prayer. Our highest communion with God comes in the worship of the whole congregation. In prayer and praise we commune with God; and in the Eucharist we participate in his life. Worship is the source of all virtues, and in public worship we find the source of communal life.

Worship is not artificial and foreign to man, but is native to him. All worship whatsoever, whether pagan, Jewish or Christian, has its roots in human nature. The source of religion is the need of man for God. That need finds its expression in several characteristic human activities; and Christianity shares with other religions this common base of human need. Because the Church is Christian does not mean that its worship is not rooted in human nature. Christianity is not alien to man, and is not imposed on him as an external thing. By nature, man needs God and seeks to have fellowship with him. The pagan religions strive to worship they know not whom, but they fail to have fellowship with God because they do not know him. Judaism knows God, but because the knowledge is inadequate the worship is defective, and the communion is imperfect. Only in Christianity does man find his peace in God. Only in the mediatorship of Jesus Christ is man brought together with God. In the perfection of the union of God and man through Christ, man finds God, and God redeems and saves man. Salvation means the restoration of man to his created birthright and the fulfillment of human life in God. In Christianity man finds God and has communion with him.

Since Christian worship is the fulfillment of our human nature, it shares much with paganism and Judaism. It is not a condemnation of the rites and ceremonies of the Church that they are similiar in certain respects to pagan rites. What of good and truth the pagans have discovered is there in their worship because it is part of God's revelation of himself in his creation. The value of Christian worship lies in its truth and not its uniqueness. Christian worship is the expression of the kind of communion which God intended for man when he made him. We should not be shocked, therefore, that Christian rites and ceremonies have much in common with the forms of other religions. God has not left himself without witness, even in paganism. But the Gentiles did not clearly know whom they worshipped, and the modern pagans only dimly glimpse the One they really need. It is only in Christianity that a true communion with God becomes possible. In Christian worship alone is there perfected fellowship with God.

If what we have said is true, then our study of each instrument of Christian worship and of each Christian rite and ceremony properly begins with an indication of the laws of nature which are involved in it. For example, if we are studying the church building as an aid to worship, we should properly begin our investigation by pointing out that all humans have sacred mountains, or groves, or temples as places for the worship of God. It is human to demand a place for worship. That tendency finds its perfected expression in the Christian temple or church. Again, all religions have holy days. That is because men as men demand certain special seasons for the honoring of the Divine. The root of the demand for holy days is in human nature; but the fulfillment of this inclination is the festivals and fasts of the Christian Church. The same is true of weddings and burials, of Scriptures and sacraments. All of them have their ground in human nature; but they find their perfection only in Christianity.

After we have studied the general tendencies to worship as found in human nature, we ought to consider Jewish worship. The Jew did know the true God, although he did not know him through a perfect communion with him. Because the Jew did know God, his worship was much more adequate than was that of the Gentiles; and so Jewish worship is more significant for the Christian than pagan worship. The services of Synagogue and Temple are a long step forward in the path of progress toward Christian worship. The Christian scholar moves from the study of the pagan groping for adequate forms of worship to the study of the Jewish worship of the true God.

However, even though the Jew did worship the true God, much of his ceremonial was immature, and a mere suggestion or symbol of what perfect worship should be. The sacrifice of animals was merely a shadow of the true worship of the true God. Man does not find God by the shedding of the blood of goats and oxen, and by the burning of the dead bodies of animals. What God requires of man is a pure and contrite heart, and a true reconciliation with God himself. The true worship of contrition and reconciliation only comes in the Eucharist, and the Eucharist was not possible until our Lord rent the veil of the Temple and, as the Great High Priest, entered into the Holy of Holies.

Christian worship cannot be understood until Jewish worship has been studied. Christian worship is the perfection of what has been truly begun in Jewish worship. However, even Christian worship did not appear in its completed form at the very beginning of the Christian Church, for Christian worship itself is a development. Although our Lord revealed God to man, he did not reveal the many possible forms of Christian worship.

He made suggestions about worship, and indicated the direction of its development; but the creation of the worship itself was the work of his Church.

The early Church soon began its task of liturgical creation; and in this work the worship of the Synagogue was the clue. The lessons and the sermon of the weekly service were modified and recreated. The seven day week was retained, but the Sabbath or seventh day was given up, and in its place the Lord's Day or the first day was made into the weekly holy day. The Eucharist became a Sunday service, with the breaking of bread and the drinking of the cup, done at his command in remembrance of him. Circumcision was surrendered, and in its place baptism was used as the rite of initiation into the fellowship of the Church. All of this is revealed in the Books of the New Testament.

The Church of the Apostles was already in possession of a worship characterized by the most distinctive aspects of all future Christian worship. In germ, the complete Eucharist is there, although not yet developed in the form of an elaborate rite. Of course, architecture was not yet utilized, for the early Church worshipped in private homes. But the beginning of a Christian calendar was made, for the Church had the seven day week and the Lord's Day. The yearly cycle was not yet developed, but the recognition of the weekly celebration of our Lord's death was soon an established custom. It was not long before there was the annual recognition of Easter. When the year found its focus in Easter, then the Church had the framework for Pentecost and Ascension. In this way, the Christian worship grew.

This further development after the days of the Apostles is recorded in the pages of the Fathers. We need patristic evidence to see how the Scriptural services grew into the elaborate worship of the Church. For example, the Eucharist was originally a simple blessing of the broken bread and the cup. These were then shared by all the faithful. Later, there came into being an elaborate service of praise, of thanksgiving, and of sacramental devotion. The elaborate ceremony revealed the drama of redemption, and made the communicant conscious of the meaning of the Communion as a participation in the life and death of Christ.

What is true of the Eucharist is also true of baptism. In the pages of the Fathers we see why the Church developed infant baptism as a reasonable and lively service by which young children were brought to Christ. The Church in her wisdom became the family of the Children of God. She was a religious community in which children shared with those of riper years the fellowship of Christ's Church. The Synagogue brought the young child into the household of Israel. Christianity fulfilled Judaism, and the tenderness of Judaism finds an even deeper tenderness in Christianity. The baptized child shares in the sacramental body of Christ.

The study of baptism in the pages of the Fathers leads us to discern an important aspect in the true development of Christian worship. It is based upon the principle enunciated by our Lord himself. He tells us, "The sabbath was made for man, and not man for the sabbath."[1] This principle which he applies to the Sabbath is valid for all Christian worship. Our Lord makes this clear by his discussion of David and the shew bread. Even though it was consecrated bread, David allowed his followers to eat it. Their hunger necessitated a modification of religious usage because of human need. In religious ceremonial the Church tempered by equity the rule of her ordinances when human necessity demanded it. For example, fast days have been modified by ecclesiastical authority when need has arisen. Since fast days are not ends in themselves, they should be used in accordance with their value as means of worship.

In the true development of worship, those in authority have been given power to make dispensations where the prescribed

[1]Mk. 2. 27.

forms of worship work a hardship. Kneeling is the rule for the reception of the Eucharist, but when sickness makes this posture inadvisable the rule may reasonably be modified by those in authority. It is a wise rule that says that marriages should not be celebrated during Lent; but there are special occasions when the rule should undoubtedly be modified. As circumstances change, worship itself should be adjusted. Equity requires that the rules of ceremony may change as the ways of life change. The rules may safely be modified if new methods lead to the end that should be realized. Feasts and fasts, architecture and forms of ceremony may be altered if the change improves the worship by man of God.

Christian worship, therefore, is the perfection of a natural feature of life. The Church has developed this natural inclination from the clues given to her through Judaism. In the spirit of her Lord, she has perfected a worship which has brought man into communion with God through prayer, thanksgiving and sacrament. But the Church must always remember that rite and ceremony are not ends in themselves, but are the means of bringing man into communion with the living God.

CHAPTER XII

PLACES FOR THE PUBLIC WORSHIP OF GOD

IF we are to have public services in honor of God, we need places set apart, appropriate for his worship. That is because human beings are only satisfied when they have places consecrated to the worship of their deity. Sometimes these places are altars in the fields, sometimes mountains, sometimes groves, sometimes grottos in the earth, and at still other times temples built as houses of God. It is a fundamental human tendency which demands that we consecrate places and buildings to the worship of God.

Among these various places set aside for worship, some are more suitable to true worship than are others. As we have seen, it is the decorous which is the test of suitable worship, and such beauty is the criterion of seemly worship of the true God. So, the idolator may often have discovered appropriate ways of worship. Many of his temples have in them things of beauty suitable to the true worship of the true God. What the idolator has used is not condemned by his idolatry. As God has not left himself without witness among the various races of mankind, and as the pagan has often been correct about the things of God, so he has not infrequently been right as to what is decent and seemly in the worship of God. Man in his search has found out many things about God; and has discovered appropriate ways of worshipping him. Because an idolator has used a form of worship does not mean that that form is therefore evil. It is only idolatry itself which is evil, and not the beauty of its worship, for God is the author of that which is good, even in things which are evil.

So much for worship as natural. The search for God was

developed under God's guidance among the Jews. They too had places of worship, for when the Children of Israel were in the desert and had no settled place of dwelling, even then God commanded them to make a movable tabernacle. Even when in the desert, they looked forward to the time when they should build a temple for the worship of God. The temple was to be built when Canaan would be theirs; and the place of the temple would be Mount Moria, in the midst of Jerusalem.

It was King David's most fundamental desire to build a temple for the honor and glory of God. It grieved him that he could not build the house of God. He knew it was no little thing to build a temple of such majesty and such stateliness as he proposed. Even though he could not build it, he gathered the materials together for the building that should be. He brought together all the gold, silver, brass, iron, wood and precious stones which he could afford to buy. As he himself said, "Moreover, because I have set my affection to the house of my God, I have of my own proper good, of gold and silver, *which* I have given to the house of my God, over and above all that I have prepared for the holy house, *even* three thousand talents of gold, of the gold of Ophir, and seven thousand talents of refined silver, to overlay the walls of the houses *withal*."[1]

The first house of God was planned by David and built by Solomon. It was destroyed, however, when the people of Judah were carried into exile by the Babylonians; but after the return from captivity a second temple was built. There were those still living who could remember the first temple, and they grieved because the second temple was inferior to the first. The times of Solomon were more favorable for building a beautiful temple, and so the second house of worship did not measure up to the first. Those who had seen the first temple wept when they saw the second because it was so much less beautiful than the first; yet even so, the second temple was the wonder of the

[1] 1 Ch. 29. 3,4.

whole world. The Jews desired that their temple be as beautiful as possible, because they thought its beauty expressed the worth and glory of God. It was David who sang, "Worship the Lord in the beauty of holiness."[2]

So much for the Jewish Temple; and now we come to the perfecting of Judaism in Christianity. Both our Saviour himself and his Apostles worshipped in the Temple and the Synagogue. Our Saviour drove the money changers from the Temple because he considered it a place of prayer sanctified to the worship of God. It was not a place of business or a mart of trade, because it was set aside as a house of prayer.[3]

The Apostles continued to frequent the Temple as their place of worship; and they continued to pray in the Synagogue. However, when the Jews found that the Christians deviated from them, the followers of our Lord were excluded from the Jewish places of worship. Hence, they were forced to find houses of worship of their own. These were usually private houses. As the times were dangerous for the Christians, they sought out not the places that were most suited for worship, but the safest places. The times were not appropriate for the creation of suitable temples for the worship of God.

During the days of persecution, first under the Jews, then under the Romans, the worship of God was not performed with beauty, and the Churches were not distinctly appropriate. There were other considerations of more importance than beauty, and so it could be said with justice at that time that the best temples for the worship of Almighty God were the sanctified souls and bodies of the believers. During the days of the early Fathers of the Church, it was emphasized that the affection of his worshippers meant more to God than any external ornaments.

All of this changed when better means became available. Under Servius and the emperors who immediately followed

[2] Ps. 29. 2. Auth. version.
[3] Mt. 21. 12.

him, there was a time of prosperity for the Church. Then the older buildings were discarded and more seemly temples were erected in every city. However, the times did not long remain favorable, for Diocletian caused the churches to be destroyed. But when Maximus issued a decree allowing the churches to be built again, "the hearts of all men were filled with a divine joy, for they saw those places which the irreligion of a tyrant had destroyed built up again. The churches were more beautiful than before, for the new builders bestowed more upon them than the original founders."[4]

There is no indication that God delights to dwell in a house of poverty; there is no proof that he only wishes to be worshipped in a poor cottage. God was as appropriately worshipped and honored in the most stately Temple of Solomon as he was in the Tabernacle in the desert. The truth is that God may be worshipped in either a cottage or a magnificent church. As the author of Ecclesiasticus says, "A man need not to say, What is this? wherefore is that? For he hath made all things for their uses."[5] This is true of churches. Both the simple dwelling house and the expensive temple are suitable for the worship of God. A man does not need to say that the cottage is worse than the temple. Neither need he say that the temple is less acceptable than the cottage. Each is appropriate in its due season. The room in the cottage is appropriate when the church is poor; the costly temple is when God has given wealth to his people.

There is a natural seemliness which should characterize the house which is the house of God. As David says, "And the house which I build *is* great: for great is our God above all gods."[6] Our love for God is revealed by the fact that nothing is too precious to be used as the instrument of his worship. The witness of his greatness is the most glorious of instruments to

[4]Euseb. lib. x. cap. 2.
[5]Ecclus. 39. 34.
[6]2 Chron. 2. 5.

express the fact that God of all things is incomparably the greatest. God has made many glorious things; he is the creator of the splendor of heaven and earth. Does he wish that all this glory be used for secular things? Does he mean that only baser things shall be used in his worship? Kings and rulers are only the ministers of God in this world, and yet royal ceremonies use gorgeous things. Do we think that God wishes to accept from us what the most lowly king would disdain?

A church, of course, is a house of worship, an instrument of praise to God. It is not the end of our lives, but a means of worshipping God. It is quite possible, therefore, to have beautiful houses of worship, and to fail in the primary purpose of religion, which is the redemption of the souls of the people of God. We may spend huge sums upon timber and stone, and never feed the poor; we may pay out fabulous sums for churches and not love our neighbor. St. Jerome tells us that the walls of our church may be encrusted with marble and supported by beautiful pillars. He says that the roof may shine with gold. The altar may be adorned with precious stones. This is not blameworthy. However, if we neglect the weightier obligations and only build churches and never clothe the poor, or visit the sick, or feed the hungry,—then the principal duty of our religion has been set aside for a lesser one. However, the beauty of worship and the glory of the temple of God are things of importance, and are not to be disregarded. We must not allow the building of churches to destroy our higher obligations, but beautiful churches are honorable works for the glory of God. God, who requires us to love and nourish our neighbor, also accepts a beautiful church dedicated to him as a work of honor to him.[7]

A church exists as a house of worship; it is the place of the public adoration of God. It is, therefore, a house of greater dignity than another house. Hence, if a church is not sanctified and treated with reverence, it would seem to mourn as defrauded

[7] Migne S. L. xxii. 535.

of its right when other public buildings are given more honor than it. The church as the place of the public worship of God should have a perfection appropriate to the honor of the All-Highest; and this perfection is impossible if the church building itself is not of the highest dignity and beauty.

True worship is always acceptable to God; and so he is more concerned with our love than the place of worship. God heard Moses in the midst of the sea; and he heard Job on the dung hill. He heard Hezekiah when he lay sick upon his bed; and he heard Jeremiah when he lay in the mire at the bottom of the well. He heard Jonah when he was inside the whale; and he heard Daniel when he was in the lion's den. He heard the three children who were in the fiery furnace; and he heard the thief on the cross. He heard St. Peter and St. Paul in prison; and, wherever they are, he hears his children when they pray to him or worship him. It is not the place but our attitude that makes the worship acceptable. However, the place in which we worship is an aid to us in our prayers. The majesty and the sanctity of the place are of great help to us in our worship, because they serve as an outward and visible means of exciting our devotion. They no doubt improve the very best worship in the world. We ask everybody to worship God, and we ask people to worship him in the assembled congregation. For this worship no place is so satisfactory as a church, and no church is so satisfactory as a beautiful church. With David we say, "Worship the Lord in the beauty of holiness."

CHAPTER XIII

THE PUBLIC READING OF THE SCRIPTURES

THE public liturgy of our Church includes the reading of long portions of Holy Scripture; and we consider this so necessary that we will not admit the use of any forms of services which do not have it. Like the other features of public worship, the reading of Scripture is rooted in human nature, was developed by the Jews, and was perfected in Christianity.

The lack of the knowledge of God is a cause of evil in human life; and the knowledge of God is a source of virtue and of our ultimate happiness. We cannot have perfect virtue without the knowledge of the good; and the good, as we have learned, is communion in love with God. The search for the knowledge of God is our first duty, because if we do not know him, we cannot love him as we ought. The knowledge of God is not the highest obligation of life, but it comes first because if we do not know him we cannot love him. That is the reason why religious instruction is necessary, and why the proclamation of the truth about God is a primary religious necessity.

If the truth about God is not proclaimed to the people, they do not know what religion means. It is strange, therefore, that although no people in the world has lived without religion, religious instruction has so seldom been a part of the public services of pagan religions. There has been private teaching of religion among all the nations of men, but public instruction as a part of the official services has been almost exclusively a method used in the Synagogue and the Church. Paganism has never made the proclamation of religious truth part of its outward ceremonies.

The Jews used two means of religious instruction in their services. First, they read the Law and the Prophets; and then they interpreted what had been read. The truth of revelation was first read to the congregation from the sacred volumes of the Scriptures. Only after the Word of God was read was there explanation or preaching. The public reading of the sacred Scriptures was, therefore, the foundation of all preaching.

It was because the Books of the Law were read aloud each Sabbath that Moses was proclaimed to all the cities of the Gentiles. Christ, when he attended the Synagogue, himself adhered to this custom. We are told that at Nazareth he read aloud to the people the portion of Scriptures appointed for the day. It was this selection from the Lectionary which he interpreted to his readers. St. Paul also went to the Synagogue and read aloud from the sacred oracles. The Scriptures were for him, as for our Lord, the foundation of his preaching. For both Christ and the Apostle Paul, the reading of the Scriptures was the fundamental form of instruction, and the basis of all preaching.

If we turn to the early Church, we find that there was an order observed in the reading of the Scriptures. First, there was a portion read from the Old Testament; second, there was a portion read from the Epistles; and third, there was a portion read from the Gospels. Both Justin Martyr and St. Augustine explained the reason for this order. As Justin says, "The Apostles taught us just as they themselves had learned. First, they learned the Law, and after that the Gospel. What is the Law but a shadow of the Gospel? What is the Gospel but the Law fulfilled?"[1] St. Augustine tells us the same thing in another way: "The Old Testament says the same thing as the New Testament. However, in the Old Testament the matter lies under a shadow; but in the New Testament it is brought into the light."[2]

[1] Just. Quaest. 101.
[2] Migne, S. L. xxxiv. 732.

When we hear the Scriptures read in the lessons of the Church, we move from the lesser to the greater, we move from the Law and the Prophets to Jesus Christ.

The voice and testimony of the Church declare the Scriptures to be the law of the living God. This is not an insignificant testimony; it is not a matter of private opinion. It rests upon the witness of all the Churches throughout the ages. From the time of their publication up to this very day and hour, the undivided voice of the Church has declared the sacred authority of Holy Scripture. The clearest indication of the authority of the Holy Scriptures is the fact that they are read as the foundation of instruction by the Church. Therefore, the reading of the Word of God to the public congregation is the plainest evidence that the Church acknowledges the authority of the Scriptures. If these Scriptures are the Word of God, their reading is the true source of all true preaching.

The advantage of reading the Bible to the congregation is that the principles of sacred truth are delivered in the very words of God's own law. Even the simplest man can learn from these words, and thus have a measure by which he can judge the sermons he hears. The Scriptures cannot be made available to the people except by reading them in public. Most men do not read the Bible in private, and they only learn to know it when it is read to the congregation. If the only portion of the Bible read is a short selection to be used as a text for the sermon, the people learn little of the whole range of the Scriptures. Men should hear much more than that which is used for the purpose of preaching; they need to hear the whole Bible. That is the reason for a lectionary providing for the public reading of the whole Bible to the congregation.

The sermon should never overshadow the Scriptures. The place of honor should be given to the Bible, for the word of God is our source of authority, and must be exalted as God's own declaration to us. It may be contended that the reading of the

Scriptures does not benefit men very much, and that it is preaching which really influences them. This, however, is not the biblical idea, for we are told in Second Kings that when the Book of the Law was lost and was later found, King Josiah had it read to him.* When he found that he had not obeyed the things commanded by the Law, he was grieved. Thus it was that the mere hearing of the Law brought repentence to the king. What was true for King Josiah is true for us; the reading of the Scriptures is the first step in the production of repentence. Sermons only make manifest what the Holy Scriptures mean.

God intends that the reading of the Scriptures should be both the foundation of all religious instruction and the means of perfecting religion. This is what is meant by Moses' words to the priests, the sons of Levi, "When all Israel is come to appear before the Lord thy God in the place which he shall choose, thou shalt read this law before all Israel in their hearing. Gather the people together, men, and women, and children, and thy stranger that *is* within thy gates, that they may hear, and that they may learn, and fear the Lord your God, and observe to do all the words of this law."'

Our Lord and Saviour himself thought that those who were not persuaded by Moses and the Prophets would not even be persuaded by a preacher sent from the dead.' It is to be granted that many people hear the Scriptures and do not believe them. Still, it is not because the Scriptures are insufficient, but because of the hardness of the hearers' hearts, for nothing will persuade them. However, it is to be granted that preaching has its own power; it makes clear the meaning of the word of God. The bare contemplation of heaven and earth cannot give us the way of salvation, because the heavens and the earth do not manifest the high mysteries of our faith. What we learn from the

*2 Kg. 22. 8-14.
'Deut. 31. 11,12.
'Lk. 16. 31.

heavens and the earth comes to us from observation and reason; but the doctrines of our faith only come to us through divine revelation. When we read the Scriptures, the mysteries of the faith are declared to us by God himself.

It is small wonder, then, that the Bible accomplishes so much, even without sermons. There is not one single aspect of the Christian faith, and there is not one duty necessary for salvation, which is not declared to us in the Holy Scriptures. We consider a result miraculous if it is produced by unlikely means. But it is not a wonder when we read the Bible and believe the will of God. At the close of his Gospel, St. John tells us the purpose of his writing, and that is the purpose of all Scripture: "But these are written that ye might believe that Jesus is the Christ, the Son of God; and that believing ye might have life through his name."[6] The Scriptures were written to reveal to us the way of salvation, and this was the conviction of the biblical authors themselves. If, in very truth, they are such a revelation, then the reading of them to the congregation is effective for instruction and reproof.

If we do not read the Scriptures to the congregation, we have violated the ordinance of God; for it is not the declarations of the preacher which are of primary importance, but the reading of God's own word. As St. Augustine tells us, devout men come to the church every day, attentively listen to the lessons that are read, go home, and then reflect on what they have heard.[7] St. Cyprian tells us what the reading of the Word means to the hearts of men. The joy of these hearers is an argument for him that the reading of the lessons is a blessing which comes as one arising from the word of life. "When the Scriptures are read to us, the word of God is certain. God speaks with us, and then we talk with God in prayer."[8]

[6] Jn. 20. 31.
[7] Migne, S.L. xxxvi. 805.
[8] Cypr. lib. ii. Ep. 5.

CHAPTER XIV

FEAST DAYS

A casual consideration of time would seem to indicate that there is nothing, either in nature or in man, which makes special holy days natural. Time in and of itself has no other character except that of continuance. It does not even require measure or motion, for that which is at rest and does not change has continuance, and hence is temporal. Motion and change, of course, do furnish us with the measure of time; but time is merely measured, not constituted, by the motion of the heavenly bodies. As the motion of these heavenly bodies is circular, our measure of time is the year, and with the recurrence of the year we have the seasons of the year.

In itself time has no quality; it only has a certain quantity of continuance. However, special days do have their basis in nature, since we do distinguish one day from another. That is because the things which take place in time have a distinct individuality, and so we attribute to the individual days the qualities of the things which take place in them. As the days of the years recur, we distinguish them by the things which have happened in the preceding years. Thus, holy days are honored because they are connected with certain extraordinary manifestations of God's goodness. It is natural for man to distinguish a day by the events which have happened on it; and there is, therefore, both in human nature and in nature, something which makes festal days natural.

The distinction of one day from another, the hallowing of holy days as distinct from other days, is not unlike the setting aside of certain places for God's worship. God is in all places, yet he does not give to all places equal honor. It is, therefore, appropriate for us to consecrate churches to the glory of God. It is also true that he works continually and at all times; and yet he does not give the same dignity to each day. As his unusual presence sanctifies certain places, so his unusual works sanctify certain days. For the man who loves God, one day does differ from another in glory. The difference is to be found in the uniqueness of the divine acts which have taken place on certain special days. These days are hallowed in memory and are quite appropriately celebrated year after year. God sanctifies a day by his marvelous works; and we honor it, as it returns again and again, by our festivities.

The honoring of certain days is, therefore, a token of our thankfulness to God. However, it is not enough for each man to have a private calendar of days and seasons in which he honors God. There is need of public recognition for the wonderful benefits which God has bestowed upon us as his people. Private reverence is not enough for public benefits. God's public benefits should be given approbation by days which are chosen as public memorials for the mercies he has shown to all men. These public memorials are vested with the works of esteem which separate them from other days. Of course, there is no quantitative difference between a holy day and another day; but the holy day is separated from other days by the worthy things which God has wrought in it.

We show regard for those days which have been made memorable by God's acts, and we treat them as holy during the recurring years. We indicate the sanctity of those days by the things we do on them. Feast days are happy days; and we rejoice in them because of God's loving kindness to us. On these days we praise God, and give him bountiful gifts because we are happy. On feast days we cease from our ordinary labors because the cares of ordinary business are not appropriate to the joys of festal days. It is clear, then, that we honor a feast day by three things: (1) our joy and praise, (2) our gifts, and (3) our rest from toil.

First, let us deal with our joy and praise. The praise that God wishes is not merely from the mouth, but from the heart. The wicked man, as well as the righteous, can sing the praises of God on feast days; but God requires of us true service and hearty devotion. The Hebrew prophets condemned the feast days of their times because of the insincerity of the worship. "Your new moons and your appointed feasts my soul hateth."[1] Appointed feasts have no value apart from sincere worship; but where there is true worship, they are appropriate.

Second, let us deal with the generosity which is so appropriate to feast days. When there is joy and praise, there should be a generosity of giving as an expression of our joy in God's goodness. We should aid the poor on these days, and this is particularly true of those occasions on which we want everyone to bless God. Our liberality then becomes an expression of gratitude to God for our prosperity, and a means of making others grateful for the blessings which have come to them.

Third, let us deal with that rest which is appropriate to feast days. Rest is the perfection of labor, and there is no complete happiness unless rest does crown our toil. By rest we do not mean idleness, for the idle man does not work, and does not receive the fruits of his endeavor. True rest is the cessation of work when our task is brought to its completion. Festal days are not, therefore, a form of idleness; they are the days of solemn festivity and joyous rest, the fitting reward for labor well done.

These days of festal joy are a foretaste of the rest which will be ours in heaven. There we shall enjoy an eternal Sabbath, for our festal days are only a hint of the celestial bliss which will reward our labors on earth. There our life will suffer from no defect, but will be a continuity of the highest perfection. Just as our ordinary work is painful and imperfect compared with the happiness of the festal days of the Church, so our life here on

[1]Isa. I. 14.

earth is painful compared to the festal joy of heaven. As we labor here on earth for the joy that comes at the end of weeks of toil, so our whole earthly life is lived for the eternal rest which will be ours in heaven. As we celebrate our earthly festal days, we gladly give up our toil, for this is an anticipation of the Sabbath rest which is heaven itself.

Nature herself has taught the heathen that feast days are a part of the worship of religion. The pagans knew that praise, generosity and rest are the characteristics of religious holidays. God, however, revealed himself to the Jews, and under his guidance they perfected this natural tendency. The Jews celebrated the many feasts ordained by the Law of Moses, but in their wisdom they established other festal days as well. They added the following new feasts: (1) the Feast of Purim, in commemoration of the unsuccessful and evil plans of Haman against the Jews, and the wonderful protection of God in the deliverance of Mordecai and Esther; (2) the Feast of the Dedication of the Temple and God's mercy in allowing this to happen; (3) the Feast of Nicanor, to commemorate God's aid to Judas Maccabee; (4) the Feast of the Capture of the Citadel, a commemoration of God's protection of Israel; and (5) the Feast of the Woodbringing, a commemoration of God's mercy.

So much for the feast days of the Jews. With the coming of Christ, the Jewish ceremonial found its fulfillment in a perfection unknown to the Law. The Apostle Paul did use all his power to prove that the Christians need not celebrate the Jewish festal days; but he did not oppose all holy days as such. Tertullian quotes him to prove that he is preparing the way for Christian holy days by indicating that the disciple of the Lord is not bound by the old ceremonial.

As a matter of fact, the Christian Church does not celebrate the Jewish feast days; even the Lord's Day is not the Jewish Sabbath. The Jews honor the Sabbath as the conclusion of creation; the Christians honor the Lord's Day as the day of the restoration of all things. Our celebrations are all connected with Jesus Christ and his Apostles. We celebrate our Lord's nativity, his circumcision, and the coming of the Holy Ghost; and we celebrate the Trinity, of which our Lord is a part. We celebrate the day on which St. Stephen met his death. We celebrate a day in honor of St. John, of St. Peter, St. Paul and St. James, and the other Apostles and Disciples. We honor St. Michael and all Angels; and we honor all the saints known and unknown on All Saints' Day. All of these days indicate the special blessings of God to us.

The reason for these feasts is the joy which comes to us in the consideration of God's unspeakable mercy; and after our toil they come to us as days of special gladness. Throughout the whole history of the Church, not only has the Lord's Day been observed, but other feasts as well. These customs go back to the time of the Apostles, or to other authoritative periods of the Church's history. As St. Augustine says, "Customs kept by all the world it is right to suppose have been instituted by the Apostles themselves, or else by general councils whose authority in the Church is very salutary. Such customs are, for instance, the celebration of our Lord's passion and resurrection, his ascent into heaven, and the coming of the Holy Ghost. It is appropriate that each of these should be celebrated by an annual feast."[2] There are times when the angels sing, "Glory to God in the highest, and on earth peace, good will toward men,"[3] and there are times when we too should sing our songs of gladness. The sun and the moon give light to the world, and make all things live; but they also set times and seasons. They make possible the recurring years, and give us the opportunity for periods of joy and gladness. Festal days are the splendor of our religion; they are a witness to ancient truth; they are times of joyous worship. They are the foretastes of heaven; they are the earthly rest which foreshadows our eternal rest.

[2] Migne, S. L. xxxiii. 200.
[3] Lk. 2. 14.

CHAPTER XV

DAYS OF FASTING

DAYS of fasting are as natural for man as are festal days. As we remember the times of joy, and as we commemorate the divine blessings, so we commemorate the times of grief and repentance. All of life is not joyous; some of it is sad. Those who live as they should are grieved by certain things, just as they are made joyous by certain other things. Virtue is in part a matter of taking pleasure in the right things and feeling sorrow at the wrong things. If we are to teach virtue, there should be times of grief for the things which deserve grief. As our joy is connected with the rest which follows labor, so our sorrow should be connected with the penitence of life.

Our higher joys are connected not only with the lower, but with the higher parts of life. Likewise, there can be sorrow which accompanies the higher parts of the mind. We fast not only to discipline our appetites, but also to increase our higher devotions, for fasting reduces pride and increases reverence to God. Fasting can be an act of adoration, and therefore we do fast in order to bring the mind to spiritual heights, and to carry it up from the spiritual depths. When our minds are on higher things, we do not feel the need of food, and when we are in the mood of despair food seems inappropriate.

Our life is a mixture of good and evil. As Philo says, "Let no one suppose that joy sheer and unmixed with sorrow comes down from heaven to earth; but these two are mixed together. . . . The Father has not permitted the race of men to be wholly devoured by griefs, sorrows, and incurable anguish; but he has mixed into human lot something of the better kind, deeming it just that the soul should enjoy sleep and a season of calm weather."[1] When

[1] Philo. *de Abraham.* c. 36.)

we enjoy good things we are happy; and when we experience evil things we grieve. When we are glad, our festal days make manifest our joy in the undisturbed mercy of God as the source of all our happiness. On the other hand, when we sorrow, our fasting and tears reveal to us that we ourselves are the source of our own misery, and they proclaim God as the one who can save us. The memory of our past joys renews our gladness; the memory of our past anguish renews our ancient sorrows. Because we are more prone to remember our joys than to recall our griefs, the Church has not only a calendar of feasts, but one of fasts as well.

If we sought God only when we were starved or beaten by a whip, we would be like dumb driven cattle. Suppose we never came to God of our own volition. Suppose we never communed with him of our own free will. Suppose our devotion to God were never so intense that food and drink lost their hold on us. Then man would never reach the highest of human life. But the very opposite is true, for when we reflect on higher things, we are quite naturally oblivious of our lower interests. We do forget food and drink, and we are carried above ourselves to thoughts about serious and weighty matters. Again, when we are cast down with anguish and our hearts are drowned in sorrow, we are oblivious of our joys. We forget food and drink, and think only of our woes. The days of solemn fast, like the high feast days, have, therefore, their basis in the law of nature. It is as natural for man to have days of fasting and sorrow as to have days of rejoicing and gladness. Fasting is a part of the lifting up of our hearts to God and of the repentance of our sins.

So much for fasting as natural. Now let us consider fasting as Jewish. Days of fasting were an ancient practice among the Jews, a thing which God encouraged in the Jewish Church. The extreme forms of this fasting led to public display and hypocrisy; but its reasonable forms were approved of by God. There are numerous examples in the Old Testament of special public fasts for unusual occasions. Sometimes these fasts were for a single day; at other times they were for three days; at still other times they were for seven days. In addition to these special fasts, there were those which recurred every year, and fell upon fixed days of the calendar. There was the annual fast to commemorate the sorrow for the fall of Jerusalem into the hands of the Babylonians. There was a fast to commemorate the sorrow of Israel at the destruction of the Temple. There was also the fast in memory of the death of Gedaliah. The first of these was in the fourth month, the second was in the fifth month, and the third was in the seventh month. There was also one in the tenth month. Zechariah tells us that these fasts were celebrated at God's command: "Thus saith the Lord of hosts; The fast of the fourth *month*, and the fast of the fifth, and the fast of the seventh, and the fast of the tenth, shall be to the house of Judah joy and gladness."[2]

Let us now consider Christian fasting. Here there are both private and public fasting. Our Lord admonishes us to fast,—"but the days will come, when the bridegroom shall be taken from them, and then shall they fast."[3] He instructs his followers how to fast, for Judaism had developed a form of fasting of which he did not approve. "Moreover when ye fast, be not, as the hypocrites, of a sad countenance: for they disfigure their faces, that they may appear unto men to fast. Verily, I say unto you, They have their reward."[4] Our Lord is not condemning fasting, but he is opposed to the evil and hypocritical forms of it.

As far as we know, the Apostles did not establish any fixed fasts. Our Lord, however, saw that after his ascension there would be fasting; he had said, "Then shall they fast."[5] There were apparently special days of fasting even before there were

[2]Zech. 8. 19.
[3]Mt. 9. 15.
[4]Mt. 6. 16.
[5]Mt. 9. 15.

fixed days; but as time went on, fixed days did appear. The first feast day was the Lord's Day, or the day celebrating his return from the dead, and the first Christian days of fasting were the annual memorial of his death. Because there could be no cessation of grief from the time of his death to his resurrection, the two days before Easter were always kept as a fast. Ignatius even thinks that no man can be a Catholic Christian who does not fast on the Sabbath of Holy Week. Later, it became the custom to have a weekly fast in commemoration of the death and burial of our Lord. Friday was always such a day of fasting, and sometimes Saturday was. At other times, Wednesday was observed as a fast in commemoration of the day on which the Jews plotted against him. St. Augustine and St. Ambrose both approved of a fast of two days in the week. They indicated that whether it was Wednesday and Friday, or Friday and Saturday, two days of fasting were valuable; and they thought that they had been instituted by the Church for man's good.

St. Augustine and St. Ambrose asserted that every Christian should fast each week, and I agree that this custom is one that the Christian should follow. When I agree with this practice, I am not deciding whether these two Fathers of the Church were right in their entire doctrine of fasts. I do not wish to decide whether voluntary fasting with a virtuous frame of mind is a medicine for the cure of sin. I am not here determining whether fasting is as acceptable to God as are other offices of Christian piety. I am not making a decision on the question as to whether the fasts are so important in God's sight that failure to observe them is offensive to him. I am not here deciding whether tears and fasts remove sin, and whether fasting procures God's mercy and pardon, and whether it obtains merit. There may be errors in the teaching of St. Augustine and St. Ambrose; but their errors do not here concern me. My general conception is the same as theirs, because their principal contention is that there should be fixed days of public fasting. They also hold that we should all submit to the discipline of the Church in the observation of the public fasts instituted by her.

The first purpose of the Church of God in having the fast days of the ecclesiastical year is to make us remember the evils which have caused the miseries of the past. If we have fasts, we will be on our guard against the sins which have caused our past misery. Incited by the memory of the causes of past miseries, we temper our minds and make them strong and resolute. In this way we can prevent our evil inclinations from becoming too strong. We cannot wholly subdue them, but we can reduce their impetuosity, and bring them under control.

The second reason for fasting is to make us frugal and hardy in our spiritual lives. This is even more important than the tempering of our inclinations, for we need a positive resoluteness and force of will if pleasure is not to melt us. We want even our children to have such a tint of constancy that they will never lose the true hue and complexion of steadfast endeavor. We shall then be like the virtuous poor who always fast, for they are the ones who hunger and thirst after righteousness. It is they who shall be satisfied, and not those who grow obese on luxury.

If we gaze on the sensual and easy lives cf those who are fat and complacent, we can see what we shall become, if we are not disciplined by hardness. As the Apostle tells us, we should be like good soldiers who put aside the entanglements of this life and endure hardness.[6] Fasts remind us that hunger and thirst characterize the truly religious man; and our public fasts remind us all of our common obligation. In the humility of the days of public fasts we praise God and are glad in his presence. We represent our sins and find our salvation in him. However, we must remember our Lord's warning, and be ever on our guard against pride. If we are proud of our contribution, it will be true of us as of David,—"I wept, and chastened myself with fasting, and that was turned to my reproof."[7]

[6] 2 Tim. 2. 3-5.
[7] Ps. 69. 10. (Prayer Book vers.)

IV. THE MINISTERS OF PUBLIC WORSHIP

CHAPTER XVI

THE CLERGY AS GOD'S MINISTERS

GOD himself instituted the ministry as a vocation which deals with divine things. Therefore, no man may undertake this vocation unless authority is given to him by God. Man was lost, and was wandering in darkness; and God provided those things that are necessary for the salvation of those who have fallen into sin. God has provided for the ministry of men who are to have their authority from him. Some of these men were given authority immediately, as was the case of the Apostle Paul. Some have been given authority in his name by the Church. The ministry is not every man's vocation, because each man is not suited to a work of such great importance. God has given authority to the ministry, which, though mediated by men, is not from men. The authority of the ministry is derived from God, for the clergy are the ministers of God.

The clergy are Christ's ambassadors and his laborers; and it is our Lord who gives them their commission, because they manage his affairs on earth for him. God alone is the father of spirits; and his Son Jesus Christ alone has purchased our salvation. Therefore, only the Son could give authority to the ministry of the Church. Not even an angel of heaven could have given the commission of feeding Christ's sheep, preaching, baptizing, celebrating the Eucharist, and declaring the remission of sins. Could any earthly authority have commanded Peter to feed the sheep of Christ, to preach, to baptize and celebrate the Eucharist? These commands came not from the earth, but from the clouds above. The power of the ministry of God makes darkness into glory; it raises men from the earth and brings God himself down from the heavens. The power of the ministry through the blessing of visible elements makes them the agents of invisible grace. It daily gives us the Holy Ghost, and administers the flesh given for the life of the world and the blood shed for the redemption of our souls. When the power of the ministry pours out maledictions upon the heads of the wicked they perish; when it blesses men they revive. How wretched we are, and how blind, if we fail to admire such great power. We are even more wretched if we know how great this power is, and yet think that any but God can bestow it.

Christ has given power to the ministry to rule over that mystical society which is a fellowship of souls, and the natural eucharistic body which knits the Church into one natural body. He has also given authority to the ministry to administer the Eucharist, and through this sacrament men are knit into one body with Christ. That is the reason why the ancients called the work of the ministry that of the "making of Christ's body."[1] This power is a character given to the clergy by God, and is known to be indelible. Ministerial power is a characteristic separating the clergy from other men; it makes them a special order consecrated to the service of the Most High, for they deal with things which others may not handle. The clergy are distinct from other men, and form a separate order; for as Tertullian says, "The authority of the Church has established a difference between the clergy and the people."[2] St. Paul divides the body of the Church of Christ into two parts. One part he calls the "unlearned," or, as we would call them today, the laity; the other part we would call today the clergy.[3] The clergy have a spiritual power that belongs to their order. Their work is that of being concerned "in things *pertaining* to God."[4]

The authority of the ministry is given through ordination; and in ordination the most memorable words of our Lord are used:

[1] Jerome, Migne, S. L. xxii. 352.
[2] *de Adhort. Castit.* c. 7.
[3] I Cor. 14. 16, 23, 24.
[4] Heb. 2. 17.

"Receive the Holy Ghost."[5] These are the words of our Lord and Saviour Christ himself, and by the *Holy Ghost* is meant not only the person, but the gifts of the Holy Spirit. These gifts are not only the power to perform miracles, but also the authority given to men to be ministers of holy things. When the bishop in ordination says "receive the Holy Ghost," he is asking that special powers be given to those ordained to make them ministers of holy things.

That this is the true meaning of these memorable words used in ordination is proved by our Saviour's commission to his Apostles after his resurrection from the dead. He said to them, "All power is given unto me in heaven and in earth. Go ye therefore, and teach all nations, baptizing them in the name of the Father, and of the Son, and of the Holy Ghost: teaching them to observe all things whatsoever I have commanded you: and, lo, I am with you alway, *even* unto the end of the world"[6] What is here meant, he expressed more briefly when he said, "As *my* Father hath sent me, even so send I you."[7]

Our Lord and Saviour breathed on his Apostles and said, "Receive ye the Holy Ghost." It is quite clear that the reception of the Holy Ghost indicated a ministerial commission, for he told them that their work was the remission of sins. He gave them this as their ministerial commission: "whose soever sins ye remit, they are remitted unto them; *and* whose soever *sins* ye retain, they are retained."[8]

Those who are ordained receive the presence of the Holy Ghost. He directs, guides and strengthens their ministry, but he does more than that, for he gives to the clergy their authority to carry out their vocation in regard to the affairs of God. The authority given through the Holy Ghost by our Saviour in his first ordinations is, throughout the ages, given no less to those

[5] Jn. 20. 22.
[6] Mt. 28. 18-20.
[7] Jn. 20. 21.
[8] Jn. 20. 23.

who receive ordination to the office and work of the ministry. Whether the minister preaches, prays, baptizes, communicates, gives absolution, or in any way dispenses the mysteries of God, his judgments, acts and deeds are not his alone but those of the Holy Ghost. The realization of this, if the clergyman really believes it, is enough to banish whatever is corrupt in his use and bestowing of the things of God. If a clergyman uses the mysteries of God profanely or carelessly, then he has a depraved conception of the Holy Spirit, and shows that in his actions. That is the thing that we all abhor in the ministry.

In the ministry itself there are two orders: presbyters and deacons. The presbyterate was established by our Lord himself. The Apostles, however, ordained deacons to assist the presbyters. The diaconate is a worthy office, but its function is secondary to that of the presbyterate. Let us confine our attention to the fuller ministry of the presbyterate. It itself has a higher and a lower form; the higher form is the episcopate, the lower is the presbyterate. The lower presbyter is sometimes called the priest; but I prefer the term presbyter. The term priest, however, has a certain appropriateness if used analogically. The Scriptures are full of terms used analogically. For example, St. Paul speaks of the flesh of fish, although fish are not composed of flesh.[*] That is because the substance of fish is analogous to flesh. The Fathers of the Church of Christ considered the ministry of the Gospel to be analogous to the priesthood of the Temple. They thought of the communion of the blessed body and blood of Christ as being analogous to the ancient sacrifices. It is not strictly a sacrifice, but in some respects it is like a sacrifice. The ministry of the body and blood of Christ may be then appropriately called a priesthood.

Whether we speak of a priesthood or a presbyterate is not of primary importance. The term priest indicates the ministry of reconciliation; the term presbyter has a more general meaning,

[*] I Cor. 15. 39.

more in accord with the total Gospel of Jesus Christ. Those who accept the Gospel are the sons of God, and churches are the families of God. It is the minister who adopts the child as a son, a son of God. The minister acts as a kind of father to the child. He acts in the name of God as the progenitor of the spiritual son received into the Church. As the minister of baptism, he is a father or elder. As Epiphanius says, "The order of priests . . . by the laver of regeneration begets sons for the Church."[10]

The whole of Israel descended from the twelve patriarchs; and the whole of the Church has descended from the twelve Apostles. Moreover, this descent is by the heavenly birth of baptism. St. John, when he saw the heavens, discovered twenty-four elders about the throne of God. Twelve of these were the patriarchs of the Old Israel; and twelve of them were the Apostles of the New Jerusalem.[11] This only fulfills our Lord's words when he said to his Apostles, "In this regeneration when the Son of man shall sit in the throne of his glory, ye shall sit upon twelve thrones, judging the twelve tribes of Israel."[12] Our Lord's Apostles are the patriarchs of the Church, and they thought of themselves as the progenitors of all the Church. This title of elder or presbyter, however, they shared not only with the other bishops, but with those of lesser authority.

There are, therefore, two sorts of presbyters, some with greater authority and some with less. Our Saviour gave a greater fulness of spiritual power to one sort of presbyters, and he gave less power to another sort of presbyters. The Apostles announced the Gospel of Christ to all nations, and administered the sacraments established by our Lord. But they did more than this; they ordained those whom they chose to the ministry. The Apostles had a power which the seventy chosen by our Lord did

[10]Migne, S. G. xlii. 508.
[11]Rev. 4. 4.
[12]Mt. 19. 28.

not have. The seventy were inferior presbyters who had a commission to preach and baptize, but none to ordain. Our Lord realized that the Apostles were not sufficient for the whole ministry of the Church.

Thus, the successors of the Apostles are the bishops, who have the power of ordaining both deacons and presbyters. The authority to give the power of order to others has always been the peculiar prerogative of the episcopate. In the history of the early Church we never read that priests or presbyters of the lower order were ever authorized to ordain. The power and the dignity conferred upon presbyters through ordination is indeed great, for through their ordination they receive the power of administering the sacraments. Thus, through baptism they beget children to God, but they do not produce other ministers as do the bishops. As Epiphanius says, "It belongs to the episcopal order to beget fathers; it propagates fathers for the Church. But the order of priests, unable to beget fathers, does by the font of baptism beget sons for the Church. However, the order of priests does not beget fathers or teachers."[18]

There are those who hold that there is no difference of order between a bishop and a presbyter. The reason for this idea is the fact that they see presbyters as well as bishops authorized to offer up prayers in the name of the Church, to preach the Gospel, to baptize and to administer the holy Eucharist. However, they do not consider the matter as they should. Although the presbyter does all these things, his authority to do them is derived from the bishop who ordained him. So, even though the presbyter can do many of the things done by the bishop, yet the power of the presbyter is borrowed from the bishop's lamp.

[18]Migne, S. G. xlii. 508.

CHAPTER XVII

The Ministry of Things Divine

THERE are many helps to the proper and appropriate performance of public worship,—for example, the house of public prayer, the public reading of the Scriptures and the ordered observance of feast days and fast days. But quite as important as these is the minister, with whom the people of God join themselves in public action, and who stands and speaks in the presence of God for the congregation. The authority of his vocation, the fervor of his zeal, and the piety and gravity of his whole behavior promote the grace of the services and act as an instrument suited to their performance.

The authority of the ministerial vocation aids in the carrying out of the appropriate offices of the Church. God has shown his favor to the ministers of the Church by giving them their office at the hands of the bishops. He has given them authority to bless the people in his name, and to make intercession to him in the name of the people. He has sanctified the vocation of the ministry by his own most gracious promise, and he has indicated that his promises are sure by the blessing bestowed on man through the ministry. This has been proved in times past, and gives us courage to believe it is still valid. Ordination is a seal and a testimony that the human instruments whom God has chosen will carry out the functions for which they are suited. The ministry is a living instrument or organ for effecting God's purpose for his people, and that purpose is the blessing of the people and the offering up of prayers to God in their behalf. The Codex of Justinian calls the ministry *God's most beloved*. They are ordained and sanctified for the work of praying and procuring through their prayers God's love and favor for the whole congregation.

The ministers of the divine mysteries are not dead but living tools; and so their zeal and enthusiasm make a difference in their ministry. Suppose they show no interest when they pray to God. Suppose they do not praise God with all their might. Suppose they do not pour out their souls in prayer. Suppose they do not believe in their own vocation and the work they must do. Suppose they do not speak as Moses, Daniel and Ezra did in behalf of their people. Then their ministry does not produce in the congregation the fire of affection for God, but instead a frozen coldness which numbs those who should burn with ardor.

Virtue and godliness of life are necessary for the highest ministry of the clergy of the Church. The work of the ministry is not merely that of teaching and instructing the people; it involves a godly life as well. Suppose the clergyman's teaching is correct but his example is bad; the people will follow the example rather than the teaching. If the clergyman does evil, then the people tend to abhor the sanctuary where the service of God is performed. Even God himself requires that pure hands be lifted up in prayer. As the Apostle says, "I will therefore that men pray every where, lifting up holy hands, without wrath and doubting."[1] Even though the ministry of evil men carries with it an authority given through ordination, and even though the sacraments are validly administered at their hands, yet those whose own unrepented sins provoke God's just indignation are not fit suppliants for mercy in behalf of others. As David says, "Let thy priests be clothed with righteousness; and let thy saints sing with joyfulness."[2]

The nature of anything is to be found in the purpose which it fulfills; and the purpose of the ministry of holy things is the service of both God and men. The function of the ministry of the Church is that of a public service in God's name, a public service as appointed by the Church of God, a service which helps

[1] I. Tim. 2. 8.
[2] Ps. 132. 9.

in the redemption of man. The function of the whole activity of the minister as minister is to honor God through worship and to save men.

Unless there is a ministry, the Church cannot be planted and cannot be watered, for the fruits of Christianity do not grow of their own accord. God's purposes are all joined together by a wonderful art and wisdom. They work together by mutual assistance and the lowest receives its strength from the highest. This we find in nature, for "the heavens declare the glory of God; and the firmament showeth his handy-work."* If this is true of nature, how much more true is it of the Church, which is the most absolutely perfect thing which God has created. It too has the same harmony as that of all God's creation. Just as in nature, so in the operation of grace, instruments are duly subordinated to the power of God's own spirit. The ministers of the Church are the living instruments of God's purpose; and the ministers should remember this. Otherwise, the minister forgets the fact that his authority is not from himself, but from God. The minister, therefore, ought to nourish the divine love in all men so that it is not the ministry that is honored, but God. The work of the ministry is to promote love among men, so that in their natural affection men no longer love each other like men but like the angels of God.

There are two types of ministerial actions which honor God and produce human happiness. One sort of action is the discovery of the meaning of the oracles of God, and that is the work of study and reading. This function is subordinate, but it helps in the more primary work of the ministry, which is the conducting of the services in the house of God and the administration of the sacraments.

There are those, however, who do not make the ministry of prayer and sacraments primary, but rather the ministry of preaching. More than that, the truth of the sermons, according

*Ps. 19. 1.

to them, is to be tested by the way in which they please the hearers' appetites. Such ministers as do not preach what the hearers desire are considered unprofitable. The opponents of a sacramental ministry acknowledge no ministry except that of sermons. If the validity of the ministry depends on acceptable sermons, and if the sermons do not please the hearers, then there is no ministry at all. Our opponents say that a minister is one "rightly dividing the word of truth."* The minister who rightly divides the word of truth is, they say, the one who draws conclusions from the text which accord with certain hearers' party loyalty. Thus, the interpretation of the Bible becomes not a means of rightly dividing the word of truth, but one of dividing the people.

To *divide aright* meant to the Apostle Paul simply the presentation of correct doctrine. The fundamental principles of the Church of Christ, according to the Apostle, were not to be doubted. To develop new doctrines out of texts, therefore, is to introduce diversions into the Church. Novelty is a thing to be avoided, and yet those who over favor sermons do crave new and strange doctrines. The Church prevents such novelty by requiring the clergy to subscribe to creeds and articles of religion. We ask our ministers to accept the Book of Common Prayer, and the provisions of the Ordinal. We also have canons which prevent the disturbance of the Church by doctrinal innovations. If any of the clergy cannot accept these conditions, they are better off outside the ministry, because the Church would not then have to endure the mischief of their non-conformity to her good laws.

We require that our teachers present sound doctrine, and that they maintain the purity of the ancient discipline and doctrine. By avoiding peculiarities of thought we all glorify God with one heart and one voice. However, those who make the sermon the only ministerial function do not wish this, for they say the clergyman who does not preach well has no lawful calling

*2 Tim. 2. 15.

to the ministry of the Church of God. St. Augustine says that willing comes from nature, but that willing well comes from grace. Now we say something similar of the ministry; we say that every minister ought to instruct and to teach; but we say that the ability to preach able sermons is not a grace which God bestows on every minister. The ability to preach good sermons is not the characteristic which distinguishes the minister from other Christian men. What does distinguish him is the authority given him by the Church through canonical ordination; and this ordination makes valid any act which pertains to the vocation of the ministry. It is the authority given by ordination and the exercise of that authority which make the minister.

St. Paul warns Timothy not to be over-hasty in ordaining ministers. The reason for the Apostle's fear is that the imposition of hands consecrates and makes ministers whether the men have the gifts that fit them for their duties or not. If the inability to preach invalidated the vocation of the ministry, then as men matured and gained this ability to preach they would require a new ordination. St. Augustine himself was content to accept as an assistant in his own church a man who was not well educated, and was not, therefore, one who could preach. What this assistant lacked, however, in knowledge was compensated by his virtuous life; and that life spoke out a message of greater importance than words of eloquent preachers whose lives were less holy.

Have all the priests since the time of Moses been able interpreters of the Law? Did this lack of ability in preaching invalidate their priestly acts? Did it deprive them of the right to perform those functions which were distinctly priestly? If we appoint a magistrate and he is not gifted, we do not say that his authority is destroyed. A judge or a governor has the authority of his office, even though he is not wholly fitted for it. So it may be unwise to ordain to the ministry men who cannot preach, but it is a mistake to think that such a lack invalidates their priestly vocation.

V. THE SIGNIFICANCE OF PUBLIC PRAYER

CHAPTER XVIII

PRIVATE PRAYER AND PUBLIC PRAYER

RELIGION is the source of all virtue, and of all the true worth of life. Our deepest desire is for God, and only in him is it fulfilled. Minds animated by religion are accustomed to consider everything they do in the light of their dependence on God. Our duties are then considered with reference to our relations with God. If we are truly religious we shape our inclinations according to our need for God. Then we sometimes adore him; at other times we bless him and give him thanks. At still other times we rejoice in his love. And then at other times we implore his mercy. All such religious desires, all such elevations of the spirit toward God, are really prayer. Every good and holy desire is then of the nature of praying.

Prayer is natural to man because we naturally desire God as the source of all goodness. God is the supreme truth, and the desire for him expressed in prayer is the acknowledgement that he is our supreme good. Since God is the ultimate and highest cause, all inferior causes are dependent upon him. The higher any cause is, the more it imparts virtue to the things beneath it. Therefore, there is no service which is more acceptable to God than prayer, because it reveals to God our desire for him as the source of that in which his own nature most delights. Prayer, therefore, is natural to man as fulfilling his need and completing him in God as the ultimate cause.

The Old Testament only makes more explicit this natural need of man for God, and the fulfillment of life in the God who has revealed himself to Moses and the Prophets. As Samuel says, when speaking of an ungrateful people who no longer desired a good government over them, "God forbid that I should sin against the Lord in ceasing to pray for you."[1]   The prophet Hosea speaks of prayers as the offerings acceptable to God from the lips of men.[2]

In the New Testament the full meaning of prayer is revealed. Our Lord makes clear the character of prayer in petitions for deliverance from adversity. It is prayer in which the soul communes with God. Even the Eucharist itself, which is the highest service of praise and thanksgiving, is a service of prayer. St. Paul tells us that we are to pray without ceasing,[3] just as our Lord had said we should pray and not despair.[4] Even the Church in heaven, like the Church on earth, spends its time in the exercise of prayer. That is the reason why the visitations of the angels to men have come most often at such times as men were at prayer.

This holy and religious duty of service to God has two forms. We can pray as individuals, and we can pray as parts of that visible mystical body which is Christ's Church. As individuals, we pray in private, in such a place, at such a time, and in such a manner as is most suitable to our personal needs. As members, however, of the congregation of Christ's Church, we also pray to God in the public services. Since a whole society is of more value than a single individual, public prayer is much more worthy than private prayer. Our Lord made a special promise to his Church, and said, "Where two or three are gathered together in my name, there am I in the midst of them."[5]

St. Paul did believe in private prayer, and yet he wished a large number of men to pray together in his behalf. "Ye also helping together by prayer for us, that for the gift *bestowed* upon us by the means of many persons thanks may be given by many

[1] 1 Sam. 12. 23.
[2] Hosea 14. 2.
[3] 1 Thess. 5. 17.
[4] Lk. 18. 1.
[5] Mt. 18. 20.

on our behalf."[6] Tertullian tells us of the great power of public prayer. "We come to the assembly in great groups, and together we form a mighty band. Our very size makes us powerful suppliants when we beseech God with our prayers. This very violence is pleasing to God."[7]

There is more consolation for us when we pray with the whole congregation than when we pray in private. Such public prayer is a common petition, and has the approval of the whole congregation. When we pray together, we hear the same things sought for with a common voice. If we happen to be individuals who are remiss in our zeal and devotion to God, public prayer as the common voice of the whole congregation spurs us to the same lively interest and enthusiasm as inspires others. "For even prayer itself," St. Basil tells us, "is not fully itself when it is not strengthened by the union of many voices in one common prayer."[8]

We accomplish more by public prayer than by private prayer, for each individual benefits not only himself, but the whole Church as well. If we neglect our private prayers, we only injure ourselves; but if we fail to participate in public prayer, we fail in our example, and injure others beside ourselves. The reason why religious people so much love public worship is to be found in the living force and the deep and reverent solemnity of publicly conducted prayer. It strengthens us when we are weak; and by means of it we give God a service of heart-felt affection such as we could not otherwise give him.

Hence, it has always been thought that everything connected with our common worship should be conducted with all the solemnity wisdom could devise for it. Our Lord tells us that private prayers should be made in secret and without any display at all. But public prayers are different; and he recognizes this

[6]2 Cor. i. 11.
[7]Apolog. cap. 39.
[8]Migne, S. G. xxxii. 493.

difference by his promises to us. Public prayers are the acts of a whole group, and therefore involve public ceremonial. That is the reason why public prayers legitimately involve liturgy, rites and ceremonies.

Our Lord thinks of worship as public prayer, and for that reason he speaks of the Temple as a house of prayer. As the angels are ministers of prayer, and bear messages from man to God, and from God to us, so the Temple was made glorious by their presence. Because the Temple was a house of prayer, it was made glorious by the angels. St. Chrysostom tells us that the angels are especially present in the house of God. Here he is only following St. Paul, who tells us to behave decently in church because we are there in the presence of the angels. Our prayers should be messages to God at the hands of his angels; and should be suitable words to be borne by angels to the Almighty.

The church, as the House of God, should be so built that it is suitable for public prayer. The church as the Christian temple should help us in our devotions. The minister who stands before God and prays in behalf of the congregation is also important. He leads the church in the prayers; and by the authority of his vocation, as well as his piety and seriousness of conduct, he promotes the public service of the congregation. The authority of the minister aids him in his vocation; for when he has been ordained, he has a commission to bless the people in God's name, and to make intercession to God in the people's name. Our Lord has sanctified the office of the ministry by his own most gracious promises. These promises have been fulfilled by the actual work of the ministry throughout the ages. The minister's very ordination is a promise that the selfsame divine love which instituted the ministry will carry out the purpose of that love through him. That purpose is to be found in the ministerial function of blessing the people and offering up the prayers of the people to God in their behalf.

The value of the church building as a house of prayer and of the ministry as an instrument of intercession is transcended in the value of the common liturgy itself. It has been framed by the common consent of the Church, and is always the same whenever it is used. If we compare the liturgies of the ancient Churches, we discover that they are all of one general type, and that the public prayers of the Church of God are not the result of mere human creation. There is no doubt that the liturgy comes from God, and is the work of his unique care and providence.

It is serious and scandalous when it is thought that any hidden and obscure place is appropriate for public prayer. For that reason we need appropriate houses of worship. It is even more serious when the individual man decides on his own initiative that he may undertake ministerial functions without the authority of ordination. It is equally as serious when unprepared prayers are used in public worship. It is scandalous when no liturgical order is observed, and when men pray what they wish and as they wish. When we consider all these things, and reflect on them in terms of the appropriate, we can see what is needed for public worship. First, we see why God so much respects the appropriateness of temples of public prayer. Next, we can see why he respects the authority of those commissioned to offer public prayers in the name of the people. Last of all, we see why he so much respects the precise appointment of the very words and sentences in which he is addressed through the prayers of his people.

"My praise is of thee in the great congregation; my vows will I perform in the sight of those who fear him."[9]

[9] Ps. 22. 25

CHAPTER XIX

Set Forms of Public Prayer

NO Christian condemns prayer, but some Christians do condemn set forms of public prayer. They say liturgical prayer is superstitious and should be replaced by extemporary prayer. However, liturgical prayer is very important for the common action of the congregation, and is therefore of the highest significance for public worship. If it is condemned as superstitious, one of the most important aspects of worship is destroyed.

Moreover, liturgical prayer according to set forms is natural; it belongs to every level of the life of men from savages to the most civilized. There is a delight in saying the same prayers in the same manner time after time in the recurring seasons of worship of the religious group. It means that with one voice the whole group is united in one supplication. Public prayer according to set forms is more usual than extemporary prayer.

Liturgical prayer was perfected by the Jews. The Jews used fixed forms of blessing at God's command. As we are told in the Book of Numbers, God said to Moses, "Speak unto Aaron and unto his sons, saying, On this wise ye shall bless the children of Israel, saying unto them, The Lord bless thee, and keep thee: The Lord make his face to shine upon thee, and be gracious unto thee: The Lord lift up his countenance upon thee, and give thee peace."[1]

Despite this divine command, let us assume that God will accept no prayers except extemporary ones, those which are created afresh for each service and in accordance with the specific conditions of the time of prayer. Suppose we assume that God is as capricious as we are, and dislikes the repetition of the same

[1] Num. 6. 23-26.

prayers day after day. Suppose we assume he is like the man who wants his diet changed every day. Suppose we assume that prayers should dissolve into mist as we utter them, and are never retained to be used again. Suppose we assume that if they are used again they are acts of magic. Suppose we assume all of this,—how can we excuse Moses? He made himself, if we so assume, a scandal to the whole world. He was not satisfied to praise the name of the Almighty in the naked simplicity of God's spirit. When he won his admirable victory over Pharaoh and the waves of the Red Sea destroyed the king's chariots, Moses did a most terrible thing. He cast his prayers of thanksgiving into the form of a hymn.[2] This hymn could be repeated over and over again, even though Israel was not again delivered from Pharaoh. This same hymn later became a part of the Jewish liturgy, and was used constantly as a prayer of thanksgiving. It became a model for liturgical prayer, and many like prayers have since been invented, and have become a part of the Jewish liturgical worship.

The Synagogue had a book of common prayer. Part of its worship was hymns taken out of Holy Scripture; and part was benedictions, thanksgivings, and petitions written by those who were from time to time leading rabbis of the Synagogue. These prayers were organized into a liturgical order. Some were used at the beginning of the service, others at the end of the service. Some were used immediately before and some after the reading of the Law and the Prophets. Still others came between the Law and the Prophets. The Passover was celebrated with the proper ritual,—a ritual that used large portions of the Psalms. Other special services were of a similar sort.

In the New Testament our Lord provides a set prayer for the use of his disciples. It looks as if he did so with the deliberate intent of preventing extemporary and improvised prayers. This prayer of his composition seems to be provided as a part of the

[2]Ex. 15. 1-19.

Church's common liturgy, and it serves as a model for the framing of other prayers to be used in the service of the Church. From the very beginning the Church used the prayers of the Synagogue, and then Christian prayers and canticles of the same nature. Such prayers of praise were the song of the Virgin Mary, now called the *Magnificat*, the song of Zachariah, now called the *Benedictus*, and the song of Simeon, called the *Nunc Dimittis*. There were other psalms, hymns, and songs, of which the Apostle Paul speaks when he urges the Ephesians to use "psalms and hymns and spiritual songs, singing and making melody in your heart to the Lord."* Psalms and hymns are not extemporary prayers, but are liturgical prayers. Hence, it is clear that the early Church, like the Synagogue, was inspired by the use of set forms of prayers and praise.

In the fifty-fifth Psalm, David says, "We took sweet counsel together, and walked in the house of God as friends."* He is telling us that when we meet together and go to the house of God together we should be united by a bond of indissoluble love. We can hope that there is such a unity of the people with each other, and of the pastor with his people, and of the pastor with each one of his people. This happens when in the hearing of God and in the presence of his holy angels there are common songs of comfort, psalms of praise and thanksgiving and common petitions to God.

The unity is produced when the people are all of one voice. When the pastor makes a petition in their behalf, with one voice they give their assent and say Amen. At other times they join together with him in common prayers. Sometimes the community of petition is shown by responses to his petition, as if pastor and people would stir up each other's zeal in the glory they show to God. Sometimes there are common petitions for the necessities of life which the pastor makes in the name of the

*Eph. 5. 19.
'Ps. 55. 15.

people. At other times, as in the Communion Service, the pastor lifts up his voice like a trumpet and proclaims the law of God. As each item of the Decalogue is asserted, the congregation asks God's mercy upon each one present, and when the whole is completed, the congregation petitions that the memory of God's law may be written on their hearts. God approves of our prayers because of our meekness and our declarations of our common weakness. And as the various items of the Decalogue are declared, he delights in our humble request for grace at his merciful hands to perform the thing which is commanded.

What joins us more together than such a reciprocal action? What adds more to our unity than the declaration that we have lifted up our hearts to God, when we have been exhorted by our pastors to do so? These prayers, in which there is response and reply, declare our common yearning, and also stimulate and excite our religious desire.

We have found that set forms of prayers are natural, for they make possible communal action and public ceremonial. We have found that the Jewish Synagogue used a book of common prayer. We have found that the early Church used an order of service with set prayers and hymns. We have found the advantage of petitions in one voice and responses in proper order. Despite all this, set forms have been described as superstitious. The reason sometimes given is that our Prayer Book conforms too much to that of the Church of Rome. The Reformation should have then removed—we are told—every vestige of Roman usage. Anything that conforms with Rome is superstitious. This seems to be the true argument used against set forms of prayer.

It is really foolish to say that we may follow nothing used by the Church of Rome, and must condemn everything used by her. Those of the Roman obedience do many things based on insights which are human and sound. The Roman Church is wise in much of her experience of men and things. In so far as she is wise and she is true about things human we should follow her. To repudiate human wisdom simply because it has been made manifest by those of the Roman obedience is to lose the fruit of a wisdom that we must have.

Those of the Roman obedience are Christians, and many insights on their part are insights into Christianity itself. Roman Catholic insight into liturgical matters has often been significantly sound and worthy of our consideration. The great liturgical scholars of the Church of Rome have frequently been our guides. Where they are wise and Christian it is well to follow them. Often, however, those of the Roman obedience are wrong. There has been a superstitious development in certain liturgical usages of the Roman Church. That needed reformation.

Where those of the Roman obedience follow reason and truth, we do not fear to tread the same steps and follow the same path that they do. In that respect we may reasonably be their followers. Where Rome keeps the ancient heritage and observes it better than others, we should follow her. This we should do even though our sympathy may often be closer to those who revolted against her. To follow the new and the worse is not the wise course if the older is the better.

Many criticize our Prayer Book because we allow the services to be read even when there is no sermon preached. We place prayer above the sermon, and often have daily offices in our churches without any sermon at all. In this respect we follow the Church of Rome. Those who support a reformation that would completely destroy the old order, wish a sermon and a minimum of prayers. The prayers would then be for the purpose of stirring up the congregation to listen to the sermon. We, on the other hand, hold that the Church of Rome is right, and appoint a service which the clergyman is bound to observe and cannot dispense with. This must be observed whether there is a sermon or not. This we require because the prayers of the public service are common prayers, and because the Scripture read is more important than the sermon expounding it.

We agree with the Church of Rome that common prayer is a duty which is fundamental for public worship, and must be performed much more often than the occasions on which we have sermons. So, like the Church of Rome, we have a public form of service for both morning and evening. These should be read each day whether there are sermons or not. We do not accept the position that we only have a service as an adjunct to the sermon. Our matins and our vespers are not "preaching services." What we have is a service of prayer, a service of public prayer. There is prayer and there is the reading of the Scripture, and it is complete even without a sermon.

Such worship is not superstitious: it is founded on human nature and the history of the Church. Two thousand years of Christian experience have found this method to be good, and unattended by evil. It has been approved by councils and laws, and ratified time and time again. It is advantageous, and is in the highest sense the best form of worship.

CHAPTER XX

PSALMS, HYMNS AND MUSIC

TRULY religious people do everything in accordance with the rules of that virtue which springs from a dependence on God; for, as we have seen, every true virtue has its roots in religion. Every duty to ourselves, every obligation to our fellow men, has its source in the love of God. The love of God, expressing itself in our communion with him, is the source of all that is worth while in life. For that reason, worship, which is communion with him, becomes the basis of all that makes life significant.

Worship quite rightly expresses itself in many forms. Sometimes we adore God; sometimes we bless him and give him thanks; sometimes we petition him; and sometimes we ask his mercy. All of these different relations of our spirit to God are called prayer. Every good and holy desire is a prayer, even though it has not the conventional form of prayer. God treats the moans and groans and sighs of men for him as prayers to him.

Much, therefore, which does not seem so at the first glance is of the nature of prayer. In the services of the Church, psalms and hymns as well as thanksgiving and petitions are prayers. Hymns and psalms are a kind of liturgical prayer which is not purely spontaneous, and is formed by reflection before worship. If all public worship were spontaneous, then our praise, our petitions, and even our psalms and hymns would be like the utterances of the prophets and those blessed with the gift of tongues. All our worship would then come by a special illumination from God, and that would enable men to ennoble the Church; but such gifts are seldom given. Hence the need of liturgical prayer.

The reason why the psalms occupy so important a place in morning and evening prayer is because they are prayers. As Dionysius tells us in his *Ecclesiastical Hierarchy*, the psalms are a "singing which binds together all the sacred rites." Since they are the flower of all that is profitable in all the other books of Holy Scripture, and since they are the expression of the soul aspiring to God, they are in essence prayer. The psalms increase our meditations and direct our hearts toward God, and so they become the source of magnanimity, justice, moderation, wisdom, repentence and patience. They are the poetic prayers of both synagogue and church. The psalms are used more in morning and evening prayer than is any other portion of the Scripture— the Evangelical hymns and the Lord's Prayer excepted—because they are the prayers of Holy Scripture, the prayers set aside for public worship.

The Jews used psalms and spiritual hymns as a fixed part of their services, and so the Jewish books of common prayer contained psalms taken out of Holy Scripture, as well as benedictions, thanksgivings and supplications. It was their custom to finish the Passover with certain psalms, and this is indicated in the Gospel itself, where we are told that after our Saviour had delivered the cup to his Apostles they sang a psalm and went to the Mount of Olives;[1] for they sang the psalms appointed for use at the Passover feast. Even at the time of our Lord the ritual office for the Passover was fixed, and the psalms used were prayers of thanksgiving to God.

If it is appropriate to use the psalms as part of the prayer of the Church, it is just as reasonable to use the *Magnificat*, *Benedictus* and *Nunc Dimittis*. They are used as often as the Psalms of the Old Testament, and they are even more important to us than the songs of David. As the Gospel teaches us more than the Law, so the evangelical hymns are more important to us than the Old Testament Psalms. These hymns are prayers of praise

[1]Mt. 26. 30.

and thanksgiving, and it is as appropriate for us to praise God with the same songs each day, as to make petitions to him with the same daily prayers.

The New Testament hymns were the songs of praise of Simeon, of Zachariah, and of the Blessed Virgin Mary; but they are the songs of praise for us as well. Just as the songs of David became the liturgical prayers of the Church, so the songs of Simeon, Zachariah and the Virgin Mary have also become the words of praise for the Church. The mystical communion of all faithful men is such as makes us grateful to God for all benefits received at his hands. These psalms contain the mystery of our salvation and the praise of God for it; and we thank him for his continual mercy. Hence, that which was a song for a special occasion has become a universal hymn for public worship. The use of them as parts of the public ritual has made these psalms and hymns a part of the common life of the Church, and has taught us how to pray.

It is altogether appropriate that the psalms and hymns be sung, because music has the remarkable capacity for expressing the inward parts of the mind. Every mood and phase of emotion can be expressed by music. Music can also woo us into a mood and lead us from one emotion to another. In the changing facets of music every virtue and vice can be perceived. Therefore, music can lead us to love virtue and to hate vice. In public worship nothing is more contagious than music, and nothing more powerful for good. Praise and thanksgiving, penitence and the call for mercy,—all of these are most admirably expressed in music. Psalms and canticles need music for their fullest expression.

Music is not merely a matter of an accompaniment to words. In itself, it has the power of expression, and can subdue, arouse, and thus express the very essence of prayer. It can draw forth the tears of devotion; it can elicit the sighs of penitence; and it can peal forth the notes of praise. Psalm and canticle, united with music, express prayer as mere words cannot.

David knew not only poetry, but music as well; and he considered both necessary for the worship of God. He not only wrote the psalms, he also prepared melodies for them. As the Book of *Ecclesiasticus* says, "In all his works he praised the Holy One and the Most High with honorable words, and with his whole heart he sung songs and loved him that made him. He set singers also before the altar, and according to their tune he made sweet songs, that they might praise God daily with songs."[2] The Church of Christ also does as David did: it too uses music as an aid to its prayers.

In church music every form of melody is not suitable, but only that which either adds beauty or enhances worship. If there are no defects in the music, and if it is completely suited to the whole intent of prayer, then it is admirable, and does much to heighten worship. Its function is not primarily to teach the intellect, but to express those holy desires which are prayer. Those men who are never touched by the music of the Church, and whose souls are not drawn forth in prayer and praise, must be persons without deep feeling and without aspiration.

If we really pray as we should, our prayer is joined with deep intention, and then our desires are the principal aspect of our prayers. However, to continue to desire for long periods of time involves too much anguish and pain. Hence, there is need of variety in the service, with something of desire and something of intellect involved; and so prayer, which is a matter of desire, should at certain points in the service give way to instruction through the Scriptures. Prayer kindles our desire to behold God, and our intellects delight in the thought of him. As we think about God, then we desire anew to pray to him. When we hear of the mysteries of the heavenly wisdom, then we are kindled with the desire for God. The man who has prayed

[2]Ecclus. 47. 8-9.

hears the words about God with more attention because of his prayer; and the man who hears prays more earnestly because he has heard about God. Hence prayer and instruction aid each other, and each is as valuable as the other.

When we pray to God it is not like making a petition to an earthly king. We know God is king, and a great king; but, unlike an earthly king, he knows what we need before we ask him. The purpose of our prayer to God is not to attempt to persuade him to do for us what he should do; it is, rather, to create in us sound religion and godly desire. The true goal of prayer is the creation in us of a right heart. Its end is not to make over God's will, but to conform our wills to his.

The purpose of our worship is the lifting up of our hearts to God. We ask him for temporal blessing; we confess to God our sins and ask for his forgiveness; we request the creation of a new heart within us. The fundamental end of the service, however, is not only the acknowledgement of our faults and the petitions we utter; it is also a continual intercourse between man and God, containing praise and thanksgiving. Between the throne of God in heaven and his Church militant on earth, the angels continually carry messages between man and God. The communion between man and God through the angels is made real through the two spiritual exercises of instruction and prayer. When the Church assembles together to hear the words of God in Holy Scripture, it is the reception of angels from above. When we pray, we send the angels into the presence of God. His heavenly words and our holy desires are the many angels which communicate between God and us. The teaching of Holy Scripture makes us know God is our supreme truth; and our prayer to him testifies that we recognize him as our supreme good.

God is the highest cause, and all lesser things depend upon him as their cause. As the highest cause, he gives virtue to all things which derive their beings from him. He is our highest good, and the meaning of our life is to be found in him. Our prayers, therefore, are of the highest service, because they express our desire for him; and our desire for him means our agreement with him in that which pleases him most, our love for him. Prayer, therefore, is our holy desire for God, and is the source of all our service to him. There is no duty in religion which does not presuppose our holy desire and love for God. Prayers are therefore the true sacrifice of our hearts, the rich presents and gifts which are carried up to heaven, and the testimony of our deep affection for God. They are the true means of purchasing every favor from God which he gives us.

Our prayers to God, when we meet together in the house of God, are so many heavenly acclamations, exultations, petitions, songs of comfort and psalms of praise and thanksgiving. In God's house we stir up each other's zeal to the glory of that God whose name they magnify. There the laws of God are proclaimed, and there is a humble request at the merciful hands of God to perform the things which he has commanded. There God speaks to man and man is filled with that holy piety which is the source of virtue.

CHAPTER XXI

Prayers for Deliverance from Adversity

SINCE God is the one "unto whom all hearts are open, all desires known, and from whom no secrets are hid,"[1] he knows all our desires even before we utter them. Hence, for him every good and holy desire has the force of prayer. Every petition is a desire directed to God for things which we wish to obtain, or which we wish God to obtain for us. It is natural for us to desire to escape from adversity, even though that adversity leads to our own well-being. Adversity is against nature, and it is fitting for us to pray God for deliverance from it, even though in his providence God uses it for our good. It is meet and it is right that good men should pray for peace and prosperity, long life and health, because the desire for these good things is in accord with our best and truest nature.

The Church in her wisdom has placed many prayers in the *Prayer Book* asking for deliverance from all sorts and kinds of evil. The Litany names a hoste of adversities from which the congregation asks deliverance. Morning Prayer requests deliverance from "any kind of danger," and Evening Prayer, "from the perils and dangers of this night." These prayers for deliverance from adversity are not contrary to the true Christian attitude toward misfortune, but are in conformity with it. The saints desired release from misfortune even though they often had to endure the calamities laid upon them. They wished both to be delivered from disaster and to conform to God's will. Such was our Lord and Saviour's attitude, for he desired to be acceptable to God.[2]

We pray two sorts of prayer to God. In one kind of prayer

[1] Collect for Purity.
[2] Mt. 26. 39.

we ask God to give us what he has promised us; and in the other sort of prayer we ask God for what is permissible, yet what may not be God's will to give us.   Our Lord's prayer to be delivered from the cup of bitter woe was of this latter kind.   Of course, it is unseemly to ask for things which are disgraceful and unholy; but neither by revelation nor by nature are we forbidden to implore that which is good for man even though God may not grant it to us in a particular situation.   To pray for the impossible is not evil, but it is foolish.   Thus, to pray that something which has already happened should be different from what it is now, is folly but not sin.   However, when the matter of our request lies in the future, and when the results are, as far as we know, contingent, we may reasonably make our request.   Such a request is good and holy, even though God does not see fit to grant our petition.

Our Lord Christ himself used both of these kinds of prayer. He asked for those things which were permissible, but had not yet been granted to him.   He asked his Father for the glory which had been promised to him,—"Father, the hour is come; glorify thy Son, that thy Son also may glorify thee."[8]   Our Lord made this request knowing that he would receive what had been promised him.   But every prayer of our Lord was not of this sort.   When he asked for the removal of that bitter cup, he knew that God willed that he drink the cup, yet his prayer showed a great desire to avoid death.   To understand this, we must consider the human will of Christ.   The divine will was in harmony with that of God the Father.   It was the human will of Christ which desired deliverance from tasting the cup and also desired conformity to God.

The human will of Christ, like any other human will, has two kinds of operation.   One of these is the inclination to the good and disinclination from the harmful.   The other kind of operation is deliberative; it desires what our intellect tells us we

[8] Jn. 17.   1,2.

should desire. Thus, in accord with the first kind of operation of the will, we all want health. However, it is only by deliberative choice that we desire a painful operation for our health's sake. It is by a deliberative act of the will that we accept a higher good at the expense of losing a lesser good. Our Lord's human will inclined to the good and tended to avoid the harmful. It also was deliberative.

Since this is so, we see that there were different inclinations present at the same time in our Lord, inclinations which were different and yet were neither contradictory to each other nor opposed to the will of God. Yet they were so distinct that they seemed so. It was well that our Lord desired to live, because it would have been well for him to have lived except for the special task of his vocation. Our Lord's desire to live did not contradict his desire to follow his Father's will. Yet it was necessary for the one desire to be subordinated to the other; and for that reason his soul was troubled. "Now is my soul troubled; and what shall I say? Father, save me from this hour: but for this cause came I unto this hour."[']

It seemed that the very purpose of our Lord's life was the reconciliation of these two desires. Never before had they been present in human life with such force and power as they were in the soul of Christ. Before his eyes was the wrath of God toward man,—death yet in power, hell as yet unmastered, and no way of human salvation left to man. On the other side were presented to him the world saved by God, the appeasement of the wrath of God by a sacrifice once offered, a conquest over death through the power of God, and the destruction of the forces of evil through the purity of his own soul. Let no one marvel that the soul of Christ was very troubled. The very thoughts of such things could only arouse unbelievable emotions in his mind. Even though for the joy that was laid up for him he must endure the Cross, yet he had to accept what he abhorred, and abhor what he

[']Jn. 12. 27.

accepted. We know that his very nature revolted against the agony that was to be his; and we know the agony from his groans and cries, his bloody sweat, and his three-fold prayers. Even though the reception of that cup was the very cause of his coming into the world, three times he put out his hands to receive it, and three times he pulled them back again. With tears of blood he cried, "O my Father, if it be possible, let this cup pass from me: nevertheless not as I will, but as thou wilt."[5]

In the human will of Christ there were two desires. One desire would have him flee from death; the other would have him accept it. That does not mean, however, that there was a contradiction in our Lord's will. There was merely a difference in the two objects of desire; and both were legitimate. Nevertheless, the desire to live had to be subordinated to a higher desire. Nature herself taught Christ to shun death; and it was natural and right for him to want to live. However, his desire to save the world made him willing to die, even though he wanted to live. The two desires were not therefore contradictory.

Our Lord's desire to escape death was not directly opposed to the will of God. It was not God's will that Christ should die merely for death's sake. It was his will that Christ achieve a certain end. Even so, the means were not delightful to God. God did not will the death of Christ, but he willed the salvation of men by Christ. That too was the pattern of the will of the Son of Man; for he willed to save man in spite of the grievous pain. In fact, it would have been a sin against nature and against God for our Lord to have willed death for its own sake. Therefore, he both desired to live and yet was willing to die.

By Christ's example we are taught that the most perfect mind may be troubled and may be clouded by the dreadful things which must be borne. Even the assurance that "in all these things we are more than conquerors through him that loved us"[6]

[5]Mt. 26. 39.
[6]Rom. 8. 37.

does not prevent our natures from shrinking from these dreadful things. It is natural for us to desire deliverance from oppressive burdens; and God himself is not opposed to this natural desire created by him in us. However, our prayers cannot obtain for us all the things which we naturally desire. That is because God has special purposes for us, in which we must surrender present joys for higher victories.

God desires all of his creatures to have every kind of happiness. It is only when there is a special work for us to do that he asks us to sacrifice any feature of our desire for felicity. That is the reason why, in times of adversity, he comforts us with his heavenly grace. It is with us as with Christ, for during our Lord's agonies God sent his angels to him as his comforters. It is natural for us to desire deliverance from evil; it is not evil for us to so wish and so desire. Like Christ, therefore, we are not afraid to pray for those things which God may not give us; and we are not afraid to pray even for those things which we know he will not give us.

We pray for deliverance from all evil, and from all adversity. We pray for such deliverance because these are the greatest calamities that befall us, and which press upon us in various ways. Sometimes we fear mere physical anguish; at other times we fear the dangerous situations that may press us from without. These are not always God's punishments, they are sometimes the spiteful hate and poisoned malice of those who oppose us. So great is the anguish of the furnace of trial that some men fall away from God because of it. The fear which is always a part of our natural response to that which is grievous causes us to falter and surrender the higher desires to the lower. The sorrow and fear of life need to be controlled; and God in his grace sends his Holy Spirit to aid us in our afflictions.

St. Augustine tells us that "in those tribulations which may hurt as well as profit, we must say with the Apostle that we do not know what we ought to ask. However, because these tribulations are hard and grievous, and because we tend to fly away from them we pray, as is natural for man, that God should deliver us from them. However, if God does not remove them, we should not assume that he despises us. Rather, we should assume that if we suffer these evils a greater good will come from his merciful hands. So virtue is perfected in weakness."[7]

Because all affliction is grievous, it is natural for us both to fear it and to pray for deliverance from it. Although much that is intrinsically good can become for us an evil, it is right that we should desire what is natural. Because adversity is against nature, it is right that we should pray to be delivered from it. And it is right, even though God wishes us to endure it. So our prayers in the Church ask for the deliverance from all evil, although we are willing to obey God's will. Our example is our Saviour's own prayer, which asks for deliverance from the cup, and yet asserts a willingness to die for the sins of the whole world.

[7]Migne, S. L. xxxiii. 504.

VI. THE VIRTUE OF THE SACRAMENTS

CHAPTER XXII

THE GIFTS OF GOD'S GRACE

THERE is no natural way of discovering supernatural laws because they do not have their ground in nature. There was no natural reason why Adam should have abstained from the tree of knowledge; the only reason was God's command. By his own reason, Adam could not have discovered this law. That was because it was grounded in the positive command of God, and that was the only reason for its existence. There is no natural necessity for supernatural law; but there is, of course, a natural necessity for natural law. The fall of man through Adam made our redemption necessary, and this fallen state of man makes the special mysteries of redemption needful for him.

These special mysteries would never be discovered or even imagined by either man or angels if God had not revealed them. The revelation of special commands does not mean that the laws of nature are not binding on Adam, and are not binding on us. Even though Adam had never fallen, he would have had to have kept the laws of nature to have become perfect. They are also binding on us, although we are fallen men.

Our first parents, before the fall, had the ability perfectly to know and to keep the laws of nature. Without the grace of God, we fallen men cannot even find out the nature of natural law. Neither can we keep the law of nature, unless God's grace helps us and unless he pardons our manifold imperfections and shows us his mercy. This is what the Apostle Paul means when he tells us that "the carnal mind is enmity against God: for it is not subject to the law of God, neither indeed can be."[1] True it is that we have freedom of the will, and are capable of doing both

[1]Rm. 8. 7.

good and evil; but sin is deceptive, and deceives us by making evil appear to be the good.

We are naturally careless, and our corruption shows itself in that self-deception which beguiles us when we should know the difference between good and evil. Only as God's grace spurs us through our reason, do we discern what is good and what is evil. Only as God's grace incites us do we perceive the good. Only when God's prevenient grace acts upon us do we see things as we ought and do we incline toward them. God's grace excites good desires, and God's grace assists us in carrying these good desires into effect. In one of the Collects for Easter Day we say, "We humbly beseech thee that, as by thy special grace preventing us thou dost put into our minds good desires, so by thy continual help we may bring the same to good effect."

It is the object or thing desired which moves a man's will; and the cause, therefore, of our desires is either the true or the apparent good. The goodness of things which we desire comes to us by the way of the senses, or is inferred by reason or is known by faith. Many things that seem good to the senses are discerned by the eye of reason to be evil. In such a case the voice of reason is the voice of God. If we follow our senses, and have no insight to reason, then that is what the Apostle calls *the wisdom of the flesh*; and such carnal wisdom is opposed to God. The wisdom of the flesh does not conform to God's law. In fact, it could not conform to his law, for God's law perpetually condemns what sensory wisdom allows. As the Book of Wisdom says, speaking of those who are opposed to the righteous man, "This was he, whom we had sometimes in derision, and a proverb of reproach: we fools accounted his life madness, and his end to be without honour."[2]

We are dominated by *the wisdom of the flesh*, and unless we are aided by God's grace, we are opposed to God's law, and are unable to submit to it. If this is true of the law of nature, it is

[2] Wis. 5. 3,4.

also true of matters that transcend reason and the compass of nature. Only faith can judge of God's revealed law, because the carnal mind is opposed to the laws revealed only by faith. For this reason, even brilliant philosophers are often the most inclined to be opposed to God. Examples of such philosophers are Julian, Lucian, Porphyry, Symmachus, and others of the same character who lived at the time of the early Church. These men disobeyed the natural law of God and derided the mysteries of supernatural truth.

I conclude, therefore, that the human will has the natural capacity of accepting or rejecting things presented to it. I also conclude that good things can be discovered if we diligently search for them, because they are to be discovered by the evidence which goodness presents to us. This does not contradict either Holy Scriptures or the confessions of the Church. However, this does not mean that I do not believe in the grace of God. I accept the writings of the ancient Fathers who wrote against Pelagius. They accept three kinds of grace. First, grace means for them the undeserved love and favor of almighty God offered to us men. Second, it means for them the outward instruction and doctrine offered to us by God. Third, it means for them God's love and kindness working inwardly in our hearts.

The first of these forms of grace is almighty God's general aid to us. It is the aid he gives us as the source of our being and the cause of all that we are. The second form of grace is a special love and favor to us. It is the revelation of himself to us as the means of saving us from our sin. Through the prophets and our Lord, God has revealed himself to us by a special revelation. The third form of grace is a supernatural aid which helps us in a way worthy of salvation. It helps us to reach happiness because we act in a way acceptable to God. The followers of Pelagius did accept the first and the second form of grace, but they denied the third form of it. They denied that God aided us from within because they thought that we of ourselves are able of our own power to do what we ought to do.

The first of these three kinds of grace is the one in which God bends down and shows his mercy to man by his general blessing. This is his general grace to us as the author of our being who constantly preserves us. The second kind of grace is the grace of instruction, the grace of God's revelation to us. The third kind of grace is that of inner sanctification. The first kind of grace is the grace of God as the fountain of all goodness; it is the grace of God as the creator and preserver of all mankind. The second and third forms of grace incline us toward God; the second informs us about God, and the third gives us the blessed gift of the Holy Spirit. Here we have the gift of baptism, and through it we receive that heavenly flame which illuminates us and sets us on fire with the enthusiasm of the grace of God. Through the second form of grace we come to know God, and through the third we come to love God. It is this love of things divine which is our eternal happiness. This inward working of the Holy Spirit is the grace which God has given us "to restrain insatiable desires, to beat down those lusts which can in no way control themselves. This grace quenches lawless fervor, vanquishes impetuous and unruly appetites, reduces excess, and restrains avarice. It causes us to avoid riots, to strengthen the bonds of mutual affection, to banish sects, to manifest the rule of truth, to banish evil doers, and finally to observe the Gospel of Jesus Christ without any exception."[*]

The Holy Spirit does all of this only if we cooperate with him. However powerful the Holy Spirit may be, if we fail to labor and to act, then nothing will be effected. The fruits of the spirit are not like the shadow that follows the human body without any cooperation of man. If the grace of sanctification worked without any cooperation on our part, what need would there be of asking men to strive and labor without ceasing. It

[*]Tertull. Migne, S. L. iii. 945.

would then be quite as superfluous to ask men to be good as it would be to request them to lose their shadows when they walk about the streets. Grace is not given us as a means of avoiding effort on our part, since we must work lest we make the grace of God unavailing. Because we cannot act without God's grace does not mean that our salvation has nothing to do with us. We cannot be saved if we allow ourselves to be indolent and betake ourselves to mere ease. Pelagius urged us to labor for the attainment of eternal life, and he thought because we must, we needed no grace of God. He was correct about the labor; he was wrong about the grace of God. If we say we need the grace of God, and hence do not need labor, we are as wrong as was Pelagius, although in a different way. We are driving out the false nail of Pelagius with an equally false nail of our own. David prays for the grace of God, and says, "Set a watch, O Lord, before my mouth, and keep the door of my lips."[4] But he also tells us how much labor is necessary to accomplish this result. In the thirty-fourth Psalm he says, "Keep thy tongue from evil, and thy lips, that they speak no guile."[5] Solomon also tells us to labor, "Keep thy heart with all diligence; for out of it *are* the issues of life."[6]

Dionysius summarizes all of this in his work called the *Divine Names*: "We will not, therefore, accept the foolish view of the many who say that Providence should lead us to virtue, even against our wills. For to destroy nature is not the part of Providence. Therefore, as Providence preserves the nature of each thing, it provides for the self-determining as self-determining; and for wholes, and for individuals distinctively, as for whole and individual, so far as the nature of the things provided for can receive the provincial benefits of universal and manifold Providence, distributed in proportion to each."[7]

[4]Ps. 141. 3.
[5]Ps. 34. 13.
[6]Prov. 4. 23.
[7]Migne, S. G. 3. 733.

The grace of God is abundantly sufficient for all. Through it, we are what we are, and through it we may become in the end what we should become. Both what we have and what we shall have is the result of God's goodness; and not one single thing is ours because of our own worth. If we do all that we can do, that is less than we owe to God, for all that we have received from him is his gift and not something due to us. All that we do when we have done all that we can is mere nothing, and is worth nothing. Therefore, let God alone have the glory because it is only through his grace that we have our power of well-doing.

CHAPTER XXIII

Christ's Participation in God

THE Church is the very mother of our new birth, for those who are born of God have the seed of their regeneration from the ministry of the Church. This regeneration is wrought not only by the ministry of the word, but also by the ministry of the sacraments, since both word and sacraments have regenerative power and virtue.

We all admire and honor the holy sacraments; and we respect them not because we render a service to God when we receive them, but because of the sacred and invisible gift of grace which we receive from God by their means. The very reality of the sacraments consists in the supernatural gift of grace which God bestows on us through them. How could any other agency besides the Church administer the sacraments, since only the Church considers them to be sacraments?

There are two features of the sacraments, their inner action and the form of their administration. It is the inner action of the sacraments which makes them necessary. We cannot understand how necessary they are until we realize what they accomplish. We say that a sacrament is "an outward and visible sign of an inward and spiritual grace given unto us; ordained by Christ himself as a means whereby we receive the same." The grace given us is the purpose for which these heavenly mysteries were instituted by our Lord; and the external ceremonial only portrays and pictures for us the inner working of the grace of God. However, we do not understand the inner power of the sacrament until we understand the grace that is given by it, and how this grace operates upon us.

The sacraments are used only in this world, and yet the grace they give us prepares us for a far better life than this. The sacraments are accompanied by "the grace of God that bringeth salvation."[1]   The sacraments are, therefore, the powerful instruments of God to bring us to eternal life; and as our natural life consists in the union of body with soul, so our supernatural life consists in the union of our soul with God.   However, there is no union of God with man without a Mediator between God and man, since the Mediator must be both God and man.   With Tertullian we say, "Because if he came to man that he might be a Mediator of God and men, it behooveth him to be with man, and the word made flesh, that in his own self he might consolidate a concord of things earthly and things heavenly, by uniting in himself pledges of both parts, and joining equally God to man and man to God."[2]

If, then, we are to participate in God, we must do so through Christ. This is accomplished through the sacraments, for they make us partakers of God through Christ as Mediator. It is as we dwell in Christ and he in us, that we dwell in God. Participation or mutual indwelling is the inward hold which Christ has on us and we on him. Participation or mutual indwelling is a mutual possession of each other through special interest, property and intimate fellowship. In the ministration of Holy Baptism the minister prays that the child, "being buried with Christ in his death, may also be *partaker* of his resurrection." The newly baptized child is to share in the life, the death, and the resurrection of Christ. In the *Prayer of Humble Access,* used in the Eucharist, the priest says, "Grant us therefore, gracious Lord, so to eat the flesh of thy dear Son Jesus Christ, and to drink his blood, that our sinful bodies may be made clean by his body, and our souls washed through his precious blood, and that we may evermore dwell in him and he in us."

It is now clear that we dwell in God if we dwell in Christ,

[1] Tit. 2. 11.
[2] Migne, S. L. iii. 932.

and we dwell in Christ if we receive the benefit of the sacraments. The meaning, therefore, of the sacraments can only be made clear if we consider first how God is in Christ, second how Christ can be in us, and third how the sacraments make us partakers of Christ.

Let us deal first with the way in which God is in Christ. God himself is the supreme cause and gives being to everything that is. As God is the cause of all other things, he gives of himself to other things. The effect always resembles the cause that produces it, and in a certain sense dwells in its cause. For that reason, the second member of the Trinity shares in the life of God the Father. That is the reason St. John says that the Word is in the bosom of the Father,[*] for as the Father is light, so the Son shares in that light. The three persons of the Godhead have their being in common: the Father generates the Son, and the Son shares his being with the Father; the Holy Ghost proceeds from the Father and the Son, and shares his being with them both. They participate in each other's lives, although each is in some sense distinct from the other.

The three members of the Trinity form one Godhead, and their substance is one; and their distinction, therefore, does not mean separation. They could not be absolutely distinct from each other because their substance is one. There are not three substances in the Godhead, but there are three individualities which share in that substance. The Father is in the Son, and the Son is in the Father; they are both in the Spirit and the Spirit is in both of them. The Son is the Father's first offspring, and he remains in his Father eternally. The Father is also eternally in the Son, and cannot be separated from the Son because their substance is one. The Son is in the Father as light which flows from light without being separated from the light from which it comes. The Father is in the Son as the light is in that light produced from itself. Because the eternal being of the Son is that

[*]Jn. 1. 18.

of the Father, and because that eternal being is the Son's very life, the Son lives in his Father.

Every being which has offspring loves that which it begets; and that is because part of the parent is in his offspring. The eternal Son is the only-begotten of his Father; and he must, therefore, be the only beloved of his Father. He lives in his Father because his Father begat him, and he lives in him through a mutual participation of love.

The Son of God became incarnate in man. Not only as Son of God, but as son of man, he dwells in his Father and his Father in him. The second person of the Trinity, the eternal Son of God, combined himself with manhood. In this union with man, he gave to man such life as no other creature besides himself has ever had. Because our Lord is Son of God, there was given to him even as man such a perfection of life as was given to no other creature. God is not in any other creature as he is in Christ; for Christ dwells in God as the Son of the eternal God. He is in Christ as the natural son of man uniquely because the manhood of the incarnate Logos is uniquely united to his deity. To be sure, all things that are created of God participate in God as their cause. Yet the substance of created things is not uniquely like that of God because as creatures we are different from God and do not share his substance with him. Therefore, the communion of the creature with God is not such a mutual participation as that between God the Father and Christ the Son.

Every created thing has its origin and continued existence from God. All things are, therefore, to this extent partakers of God: they are his offspring and his influence is in them. The personal wisdom of God is the cause of every creature, and it penetrates into everything which it produces. For this reason, the *Book of Wisdom* says of the spirit of wisdom, that it is "ready to do good, kind to man, stedfast, sure, free from care, having all power, overseeing all things, and going through all understanding, pure, and most subtle, spirits. For wisdom is more moving than any motion: she passeth and goeth through all things by reason of her pureness."[4] This same Spirit of God is the Divine Providence which supports and sustains all things.

When God acts, all three persons of the Trinity are involved in that action. In this section, the Father has the priority, the Son comes next, and the Spirit is last. Hence, it is the Father who has priority in creation, and bears more impress upon creation. Yet, all three are involved in the divine action. The persons of the Trinity are so inseparable that whatever one does is done by all three of them because each is the partaker of the other two. Whatever creative act, whatever providential act is wrought by God, all three persons share in that act. The Father is goodness, the Son is wisdom, and the Holy Ghost is power. The goodness of God incites God to activity; the wisdom of God arranges the plans of his works; the power of God carries it out into operation. Those things which God has wrought were eternally in God, and when they were wrought, were carried into operation as the outward result of that which is in God. In this respect, God is like an artisan who carries out his plans when he builds. Therefore, this present world which God has created was enfolded within the affectionate thought of the divine mercy, was written in the book of eternal wisdom, and was held in the hands of omnipotent power before the foundations of the world were ever laid. God the Father, God the Son, and God the Holy Ghost are all involved in every act of God. They mutually dwell in each other, and act together as one. So, also, all created things as the creatures of God's mercy, wisdom, and power, share in him as their highest cause. He is in them and he is their very life.

[4]Wis. 7. 23, 24.

CHAPTER XXIV

Our Participation in Christ

GOD is the source of our being. We are his offspring, and apart from him we cannot continue to exist. Therefore, he is the providential source of our existence. However, there is another power which we may receive from God, for as many as receive Christ are given the "power to become the sons of God."[1] "Behold, what manner of love the Father hath bestowed upon us, that we should be called the sons of God."[2]

Apart from grace, and by nature, we are the sons of Adam. When God created Adam he created all of us; and since we are all descended from Adam, we have the same nature as Adam had. Adam was not the son of God, but merely the offspring of creation; and that is true as well of us who are Adam's descendents. We become sons of God only by God's grace and favor. We are sons of God because we are by spiritual and heavenly birth the progeny of the second Adam; and the second Adam is God's only-begotten Son. As St. Paul says, "The first man *is* of the earth, earthy: the second man is the Lord from heaven."[3] God has always loved his Son, and he loves and prefers before everyone else those who have their spiritual descent from his only-begotten Son. "Blessed *be* the God and Father of our Lord Jesus Christ," says the Apostle, "who hath blessed us with all spiritual blessings in heavenly *places* in Christ: according as he hath chosen us in him before the foundation of the world. . . ."[4] Those who abide in Christ because they have sprung from him, abide in God as their Saviour and as their Creator.

[1] Jn. I. 12.
[2] I Jn. 3. I.
[3] I Cor. 15. 47.
[4] Eph. I. 3, 4.

Those whom God intended to save through their adoption or rebirth in Christ participate in God as the Creator and Redeemer of their lives. It is true that all life as well as all other gifts to us have their origin in God the Father. However, they do not come to us except through the Son; and they only come from the Son through the Spirit. That is the reason why the benediction said by the Apostle to the Church in Corinth is a blessing of the triune God. "The grace of the Lord Jesus Christ, and the love of God, and the communion of the Holy Ghost, be with you all."[5] St. Peter summarizes this by telling us that we should be "partakers of the divine nature."[6]

We are in God through Christ, because it was the divine intent and purpose which chose us before the worlds were made. Even before creation God knew what each one of us would be, and bore us a love from everlasting. However, we do not become his sons until we are actually regenerated by baptism and adopted into the body of his true Church and made members of the fellowship of his children. He knows his Church and he loves it, and those who are in the Church are known to be his children. The eternal foreknowledge of God only becomes real through actual adoption into the fellowship of the saints in this present world. It is only as we are actually incorporated into that society which has Christ as its head that we participate in him. Because of our mystical participation in him, we are in him just as much as if our very flesh and bones were a part of his physical body. As the Apostle says, "We are members of his body, of his flesh, and of his bones."[7]

We dwell in Christ because he knows us and loves us as parts of himself; and we are in him only as he is in us. That is the reason why St. John says, "He that hath the Son hath life; *and* he that hath not the Son of God hath not life."[8] Again, he says,

[5] 2 Cor. 13. 14.
[6] 2 Pet. 1. 4.
[7] Eph. 5. 30.
[8] 1 Jn. 5. 12.

"I am the vine, ye *are* the branches: He that abideth in me, and I in him, the same bringeth forth much fruit."[9] We become the adopted sons of God by participation in the only-begotten Son of God; and it is his life which is the source and the cause of our life. As our Lord says, "Because I live, ye shall live also."[10]

There are some men who say that our participation in Christ means that he has the self-same nature as all men, and because he shares this nature with us, we in that sense participate in him. This is an insipid and colorless interpretation of our participation in Christ, for it means that every man as man is in communion with Jesus Christ. But actual communion with Christ is much more rich in meaning than that. By nature we are only in our first parents; only by grace are we in Christ. We are in Christ as Eve was in Adam. God made Eve out of a rib of Adam; and he made the Church out of the very flesh, the very wounded and bleeding side of the Son of man. Our Lord's crucified body and his shed blood are the true elements of that heavenly being; and because we share in his body and his blood, we share in Christ. Adam said of Eve, that she was the flesh of his flesh and the bone of his bones. Our Lord may say the same of us, for we become a portion of his own body. As branches, we come from the root and vine which is Christ.

Because he is the Son of God, Christ is the life and the light of all things which exist. Because as Son of God Christ was made man for us, he is the eternal life and the eternal light of all those who are the Church. Adam is the original cause of our nature, and the source of that corruption which results in death. Christ is the true cause of our restoration to life. The person of Adam is not in us, but the nature of Adam is; and as Adam's nature was corrupted, we share in that corruption through inheritance. Christ also shared in Adam's nature as we do; but it was an incorrupt nature. Through his own person he gave

[9]Jn. 15. 5.
[10]Jn. 14. 19.

incorruption to our nature, and through our participation in Christ our corruptible nature becomes incorruptible. We partake of the body of sin and death from Adam, and unless we are partakers of Christ and really have his spirit, all talk of eternal life is a mere dream.

Christ sanctified his own flesh, and he did this as God by bestowing the Holy Ghost on his manhood; but he received the Holy Ghost as man. All of this he did for our sakes, and not for his own sake. He did it so that the grace of sanctification received in him might pass from him to the whole human race. As malediction came from Adam to all mankind, so benediction came from Christ to all mankind. Because we are the heirs of Adam, and because through Adam we are the heirs of sin and death, the Holy Spirit could not work upon us unless we shared in Christ. In order that we may be sanctified and have a new life in this world, and a restoration of our bodies in the resurrection, we must participate in the grace of his body and blood. Without this sharing in his divine humanity, the other operations of the spirit of Christ cannot take place. It is clear, therefore, that Christ imparts himself by degrees. First, we share in his divine humanity; and then we share in the further gifts of his grace.

The Apostle tells us that the body of Christ is "the fulness of him that filleth all in all."[11] Because of our Lord's mercy he counts himself incomplete without us. However, we receive of his fulness because he is the source and the active cause of our fuller life. As we are incorporated in Christ, the effects of his life in us really exist. They are of various kinds and degrees; and they all lead to our eternal happiness. Of course it is true that Christ is the creator and the providential governor of the world. As creator, he is the source of the being of every creature, and in this sense every creature partakes of him; but it is another matter when we partake of Christ as Saviour. Then we

[11]Eph. 1. 23.

receive his fulness and become the sons of God, sons saved to eternal life.

As Christ does not dwell in all as Redeemer, so his divine activity is not the same in everyone in whom he abides. As St. Augustine says, "This is the reason why some men are holier than others, and why God dwells more plentifully in some men than in others."[12] The participation in Christ, which makes possible a difference of degree, consists in the actual effect of both natures of Christ upon us. So we say that he imparts himself to us as the grace that he gives us really becomes effectual in our lives. It is true, of course, that Christ as Creator is equally present in every man; but it is also true that Christ as Redeemer imparts himself by degrees as the graces which come from him become more and more effectual.

Christ is whole in the whole Church; and he is whole in every member of the Church. His person cannot be divided, and can not be possessed in part or in degree. When he is present he is present in his whole person. However, participation in Christ involves not only the presence of Christ's whole person, and the presence of the whole Christ in communion with the members of the whole Church, but his actual influence on the members incorporated into him. We participate in him as his actual influence becomes effectual in a godliness which is his. As the Apostle says, "I live; yet not I, but Christ liveth in me: and the life which I now live in the flesh I live by faith of the Son of God, who loved me, and gave himself for me."[13] It is from Christ that we receive those perfections which make up our eternal happiness; but his grace becomes effectual by degrees, and some men are much more holy than others because Christ lives more effectually in them than in others.

[12]Migne, S. L. xxxiii. 838.
[13]Gal. 2. 20.

CHAPTER XXV

The Sacraments and our Participation in Christ

WE now see how the Father is in the Son, and the Son is in the Father. We see how both the Father and Son are in all things and all things are in them. We see what is the communion that Christ has with his Church, and how each member of the Church dwells in him. We see how each member is present in him through the gift of the Holy Ghost. The Holy Ghost is received by each member from him, and also each member receives the vital force of Christ's body and blood. By steps and degrees, each member receives some measure of the divine grace, and gradually receives the full measure of that grace which sanctifies and saves. The completion of our sanctification and salvation through his grace comes with the final exaltation of fellowship with him in glory. We are now partakers of him, and are by this fact partaking of those things which lead to glory.

The sacraments, as outward and visible signs, are marks of distinction which separate God's very own from strangers. Their chief force and virtue as signs consist in the fact that they are signs of grace given; they indicate that God has imparted the vital and saving grace of Christ unto all those who are capable of receiving it. As St. Augustine says, "If it be of the essence of sacraments to be signs and indications, then, where you find that God ordains them, you find that he ordains them to this end."[1] The sacraments are not only signs of grace given; they are also the inward and spiritual grace which God imparts to men. If the sacramental elements signify grace, and God is the giver of that grace, then the sacramental elements are used as

[1] Migne, S. L. xlii. 356-7.

11

the means of telling us when God has given his grace, and what grace he has given us.

God himself is invisible, and we cannot see his acts. Therefore, when God in his wisdom thinks it well that we notice his gracious presence, he gives some clear and visible indication of his special operations. It was impossible for Moses to see God and live. Yet, by the fire which flamed out of the bush, Moses knew that God was present in that place in an unusual way. No one saw the angel through whose instrumentality the pool of Bethesda had the supernatural virtue to heal, yet the angel's presence was known by the troubled movements of the waters.[2] The Apostles knew by the tongues of fire upon their heads that the Spirit was upon them, although they could not see the Spirit. So it is with us also, for we too are unable to see the Holy Spirit and Christ, and the happy results of their presence. They come into the soul of man, we know not how. Yet we do know when they make their entrance into the life of man, because it has pleased almighty God to tell us by means of the sacraments about the blessings which would otherwise be incomprehensible.

The Christian sacraments are sacraments of grace given by God to man. They are outward and visible signs, and at the same time they are an inner grace bestowed. They are uniquely connected with Jesus Christ because they were instituted by him as the means of communication with God through him. Therefore, we must understand the sacraments are the means of communication with God through Christ as mediator. They are means of grace; that is, they are the means of obtaining God's kindness to us. But they are means of grace dependent upon the mediatorship of Jesus Christ.

There is, to be sure, a very broad use of the term sacrament. In that sense, any admirable thing done in the Church and accompanied with God's grace is a sacrament, and in this sense the sacraments are God's secrets. They are the secrets disclosed

[2] Jn. 5. 4.

only to God's own people. The term is thus used by Tertullian and Augustine among the Fathers.[*] But the term is also used in a narrower sense; and then it means that which is required of man as the means of obtaining that saving grace which God bestows. A sacrament in this sense is connected with the bestowal of God's redemptive grace. There are several factors involved in the notion of the sacrament in the stricter sense. First, sacraments are perpetual duties required of men; second, they are inseparably connected with Jesus Christ as their author and the source of their grace. Third, they are required of men as the usual means of salvation; and fourth, they are the means of grace working upon those who receive them. Fifth, they involve a visible sign and an inward gift of grace. Sixth, although they are foreshadowed in the natural sacraments and in the Jewish sacraments, they are revealed in the New Testament as supernatural means which are known only through New Testament revelation. They are there revealed as the means of our participation in Christ.

The only rites which fulfill these requirements are baptism and the Eucharist, because these are the only ones required by our Lord for men's salvation, and the only ones in which he has declared that he himself, through the Holy Spirit, gives us saving grace.[*] Although there are many other gifts of God's mercy and kindness promised in the New Testament, these are the only ones necessary for the initiation and continuity of our redemption, the only ones necessary for participation in him. As a mere matter of definition, the New Testament reveals baptism and the Lord's Supper as sacraments in the truest sense of the word. Although there was baptism before our Lord commended it, the baptism of John did not bring the gifts of the Holy Ghost; and although there was a passover before the

[*]Tertull. lib. v. *Contra Marc.* c. i&c. iv.; Migne, S. L. xlii. 616 & 636.
[*]Mk. 16. 16; Jn. 3. 5; Jn. 6. 53-57.

Eucharist was instituted, the Jewish Passover did not bring redemptive salvation and participation in Christ.

The Apostle Paul makes manifest the supremacy of baptism and the Lord's Supper.[5] However, he only carries out what is manifest in the Acts of the Apostles, where it is said that the continuity of the life of the Church, initiated by baptism, is continued by the breaking of bread.[6] The Christians were first baptized, and then found a fellowship in the breaking of bread and in prayer.

That this was the conception of the Fathers of the Church was shown by the fact that they speak of the limited number of Christian sacraments compared to the Jewish ones. St. Augustine in particular speaks of this fact and exalts baptism and the Eucharist as sacraments which "have flowed out of the side of Christ."[7] By this imagery he means that the water which flowed from our Lord's side symbolizes baptism, and the blood symbolizes the Eucharist. It does not make much difference whether we use the word sacrament in a very broad way if we only remember that baptism and the Eucharist are sacraments *par excellence*, and that upon them the grace of Jesus Christ and his gifts to us are more particularly dependent.

In a sacrament there are two factors: there is the outward and visible sign, and then there is also the mysterious grace signified and expressed by the visible elements. Thus, the reality of the sacraments is the grace conveyed, and the signs are a revelation of that grace conveyed. If we think of a man as a body animated by a soul, we can say that he is a symbol or analogy of what a sacrament really is. The outward elements or signs are the body of a sacrament; and the inward grace is the soul of a sacrament. In this sense, a sacrament involves an invisible grace given and the visible elements of the rites. Sometimes, how-

[5] Rm. 6. 4; Eph. 4. 5; 1 Cor. 11. 23-29.
[6] Acts, 2. 41, 42.
[7] August. *de Doctr. Christ.*, Migne, S. L. xxxiv. 71.

ever, the visible elements and words are termed the sacrament. Then the sacrament becomes the *outward and visible sign of an inward and spiritual grace.*

In baptism we use water, and make the declaration of baptism in the name of the Trinity. In the Eucharist we use bread and wine and use the words of institution. These are outward and visible signs, but they are not the whole of the sacrament. The sacrament also includes the grace received. Thus, in the sacraments God and man cooperate: God and man here meet. The clergyman working with God brings grace to the one who receives it. The minister applies the sign which tells of the work of the Spirit which is joined to the rite. The action is God's action, and yet man cooperates with God in requesting God's grace and revealing God's grace. God gives grace through the outward ministry of man. At man's request God grants grace to the soul, and this he does directly and without instrument or co-agent. God alone redeems in baptism; and God alone forgives and unites the soul to himself in the Eucharist. Yet he does it at the request of man, and allows his ministers so to cooperate with him that they reveal in the sacramental signs of baptism and in the sacramental signs of the Eucharist the grace which God is giving at man's request.

This does not mean that the signs are mere memorials; they are the revelation and expression of the works of grace actually done. But the sign in itself is not the instrument of redemptive grace; the grace of the sign is to be found in its power to declare what God is secretly working through his grace. The outward visible signs, however, are not the instruments by which this grace is conveyed. To use scholastic language, they are not the physical instruments of producing grace, for that is done directly by God. But the signs do bring men to consider the omnipotent power of God; and without them the fact that this power was working would not be noticed.

Therefore, when his ministers do request him, God does bestow his heavenly grace. And when it is bestowed, he allows his ministers to declare this bestowal by the signs which declare it. Baptism and the Eucharist are always accompanied by this power of God; and, therefore, the outward sign is also God's instrument. It is a moral instrument; it is a persuasive instrument; it is a declaration of the inner grace which is the soul of the sacrament. The outward sign of the sacrament does nothing of itself unless God blesses and sanctifies it. God associates himself with man's sacramental act, and then gives to us the direct blessings of his spirit. He associates himself with the outward sign by allowing it to declare the invisible operation of his grace.

Can we say, then, that because the sacrament is effectual, it is magical? Because God answers man's prayers and gives the gifts of his grace, is it magic when he reveals through the elements and words of a sacrament that his most glorious spirit is really doing what the signs of a sacrament say he is doing? The administration of the sacraments is in the hands of mortal men. The ministry of the clergy is a ministry of administration. Through it there is the prayer for God's grace and the use of the signs of God's grace. When these are so used, God cooperates with man and gives the gifts of his spirit. In the sacraments the personal instruments and the signs do not work in their own behalf; but rather, the minister works with God at God's command. Our Lord has commanded his ministers to baptize all nations.[8] He has commanded his ministers to break the bread and deliver the cup in his name.[9] It is at God's request that the clergy show forth the mighty works which he himself is doing, but which they are declaring and requesting at his command. The action is one; it is God's act. But man cooperates with God in doing God's works for God and with God and under God. God gives his grace through the outward ministry of man. He authorizes his ministers to apply the sacraments of grace to the soul. God then does his own work without instrument, or any agent except his own power.

[8] Mt. 28. 19.
[9] Lk. 22. 19; 1 Cor. 11. 24, 25.

VII.   BAPTISM AND THE EUCHARIST

CHAPTER XXVI

The Sacrament of Baptism

IT is the soul which organizes the body and gives every member of it the character which is expedient for it to have; and it is the inward grace of a sacrament which determines its most appropriate external form. The soul is more important than the body, but cannot function through the body unless the organs of the body are appropriate. In the same way, the inward grace is the important part of the sacraments, but the appropriate outer forms cannot be neglected. The grace given by God is the cause of the choice of those sacramental elements which are appropriate for the expression of the nature of the inner grace. The inner grace does not depend upon the natural force of the elements. Therefore, the only significance of the elements lies in the expression of the meaning of the grace given. That is the reason why the elements must be the appropriate ones to express the grace given; and that is the reason why the words used must be taken from the mouth of our Lord himself, which will make perfectly clear what the meaning of the sacrament is.

The inner character, the invisible grace given, is the soul or inner character of the sacraments; and the elements used are like the organs of a body animated by the soul. As St. Gregory the Great says, "A sacrament is that by which under cover of visible things divine power secretly works salvation."[1]

If we treat the elements and the words used as the sacrament, then its function is the appropriate expression of the meaning of the grace given; and that, in fact, is St. Augustine's way of defining a sacrament. He says, "A sacrament is a sign which effectually signifies what is being wrought by God's grace."[2] If

[1]Migne. S. L. lxxxii. 255.
[2]Migne, S. L. xxxiii. 205.

we include in the meaning of a sacrament the grace of God given, then we have a wider use of the term sacrament, and that is the one we used at the beginning of this chapter. Then our definition would be that of Isador, "We have a sacrament when a visible thing produces something inward which is quite different and which is invisible."[8]

The importance of these definitions is that they make clear the significance of the grace of God and the necessity of the sacramental word and the sacramental elements being appropriate to the grace given. If we understand the nature of the inward grace given, and the necessity of appropriate sacramental elements and words, then we understand the sacraments. The grace given is necessary for salvation, and the appropriate words and elements are necessary conditions for the expression of the meaning of the sacraments. These are required as the appropriate conditions for the giving of the sacramental grace.

The sacraments are the work of men who are ministers of the Church. Since we cannot know the mind of the minister as he performs the rites of the sacrament, we must suppose that the minister of the Church is serious in his intentions when he celebrates the sacraments. Since we cannot know his mind, we must suppose that he is intending to perform the ministry of the Church of God. It is the Church's intention in baptism, and not the clergyman's, which makes it valid.

The prayers, the lessons, the sermons, and the many manual acts are merely accessory aspects of the rite of baptism. These are features which the Church of Christ has added to carry out the primary characteristics of baptism. The sacrament does not depend on them; but their meaning depends on the sacrament. They are not the substance of the rite of baptism, and the rite itself is more necessary than any incidental feature of it. That is the reason why the Digest of Justinian allows the performance of the rite even when all the ordinary features which add to its

[8]Etymol. lib. I.

solemnity are lacking. It is better to use the opportunity when it is present than to wait until that opportunity is lost. "Although no change," says the Digest, "is likely to be made in the administration of ritual solemnity, yet when plain equity demands it, there may be relaxation."⁴ Therefore, it is reasonable to assume that if the full ceremonial of baptism is not possible, it is better that a man should be baptized with minimum form than suffered to depart this life without baptism at all.

There are some people who say that baptism is not necessary. They admit that the baptism of the Holy Spirit is necessary, but they say that the baptism by water is not. In the passage which reads, "Except a man be born of water and of the Spirit, he cannot enter into the kingdom of God," the critics of the necessity of a rite of baptism tell us that *water and spirit* mean simply *spirit*. They say that the meaning is exactly the same as when we are told that we must be baptized *with the Holy Ghost and with fire*,⁵ for, they say here, fire only indicates the way in which the Holy Ghost operates.

The general voice of antiquity, however, agrees that water must be taken quite literally in our Lord's command. It is a wayward innovation and a sheer novelty which would dry up the water of the rite of baptism in the name of the Holy Ghost. If there is not good reason for grievous reformation, we must accept uniform testimony of antiquity as our guide. The law of Christ speaks of two things necessary for the sacrament of baptism: one, water, and the other spirit. The use of water is our duty, and spirit is God's gift. There is a danger that we may avoid our duty and treat it as if it were superfluous. We may try to do this by clever exegesis, but such cleverness proves but sorry advice.

When the Apostles were baptized by the Holy Ghost, there was a visible descent of fire, as well as a secret infusion of the

⁴Digest, 17th titulus of Book L.
⁵Lk. 3. 16.

Holy Ghost. They had previously been baptized by the baptism of John, but the fire was the visible element of the baptism of the Holy Spirit. This new baptism, in which the Holy Spirit came upon them, was certified by tongues of flame on their heads. So it is with us, for the heavenly work of our new birth is certified by the water used. We are baptized not alone with the Spirit, but with water, and our Lord's own deeds are the exposition of his words. He baptized with water and also gave the infusion of his spirit.

Let us see in what sense baptism by water is necessary. Everything that happens has a cause or a means which produces it. According to Aristotle, necessity means that which is needful for a great good or for the avoidance of a great evil. Thus, regeneration is needful for eternal life, and that is what our Lord taught Nicodemus. "Verily, verily, I say unto thee, Except a man be born again, he cannot see the kingdom of God."[6] And he tells us almost at once what makes regeneration possible. "Verily, verily, I say unto thee, Except a man be born of water and *of* the Spirit, he cannot enter into the kingdom of God."[7]

The Spirit is a necessary inward cause of our regeneration, the water is a necessary outward cause. Both Spirit and water are necessary. Why are we taught that God purifies and cleanses his Church with the washing of water?[8] Why does the Apostle of Christ call baptism a "washing of regeneration"?[9] Why does the Apostle Peter advise outward baptism as availing for the remission of sins?[10] "Then Peter said unto them, Repent, and be baptized every one of you in the name of Jesus Christ for the remission of sins, and ye shall receive the *gift* of the Holy Ghost."[11]

[6]Jn. 3. 3.
[7]Jn. 3. 5.
[8]Ephes. 5. 26.
[9]Tit. 3. 5.
[10]1 Pet. 3. 21.
[11]Acts, 2. 38.

However, outward baptism has not the absolute necessity which inward baptism has, because God may give his inward baptism without outward baptism. Now, if baptism by water were the absolutely necessary cause, then the grace of God would never cause regeneration without baptism. This we know is not true. That is what Hugo means when he says, when speaking of the outer signs of the sacrament, "The faithful do not seek salvation from them, although they seek it in them. . . . For they do not give what is given to them."[12]

Our Lord instituted outward baptism not only as a sign of the gifts which we receive from the Holy Ghost, but as a condition of the receipt of the Holy Ghost. We are baptized by water as well as the Holy Ghost, for the water is the usual condition of our regeneration by the Holy Spirit. When we are baptized by the Holy Spirit, we are cleansed of all former guilt by imputation, and there is infused into us the divine virtue of the Holy Ghost. The divine virtue regenerates us, and gives us the first disposition towards a future newness of life. As St. Cyprian says, "For not only does baptism give remission of our former sins, but it begets in us a hope of the gracious promises, and makes us sharers of the Lord's death and resurrection, and grants us participation in the gift of the Holy Spirit."[13]

[12]Migne, S. L. clxxvi. 320.
[13]Migne, S. G. lxxxiii. 512.

CHAPTER XXVII

INFANT BAPTISM

IN the public form of baptism the *Prayer Book* provides a service in which the infant child answers questions through sponsors. This use of sponsors is the ancient tradition of the Church, and at no time has the Church failed to use these questions on the ground that they were needless in the solemn baptism of infants. Boniface was a bishop at the time of St. Augustine. He knew that the Church everywhere asked these questions when it baptized infants, and he wanted to learn from St. Augustine the reason for their use. "If," he said, "I should bring a young child and set him before you, and if I should ask you whether the child would be honest and just when he grows up, you would tell me that no man can know what the future of the child will be. Again, if I should ask you whether the child was conscious of good or evil, you would tell me you do not know what he now thinks or what he will do in the future. Yet the parents do promise what the child will do in the future. Therefore, they promise in the child's name what it is impossible to promise. Tell me, therefore, by what authority we have this custom, and what is the reason for it?"[1]

St. Augustine says that in a special sense an infant can believe at the time of its baptism. Of course, there is no actual habit of faith in the child himself; but the sponsor or parent affirms a faith which can become the faith of the child in the future years. By so doing, the sponsor has taken the first step in creating the habit of faith in the child. It is the seed sown in life which will produce fruitage later. Even though the child does not understand what is affirmed for him, this is the first step to what may be later acknowledged with understanding.

[1] Migne, S. L. xxxiii. 363.

We are now believers because at some time we began that process of belief which is now perfected in us; and until we come to actual belief, baptism as a sacrament of faith acts as a shield of protection against all contrary infernal powers. Anyone who denies this possibility is further removed from the Christian faith than the infants themselves. Even though the infants do not have an active faith, they are at least untouched by the denial of the faith, whereas those who deny the possibility of the growth of the faith in children are not even untouched by doubt. We often call men believers because they make an outward profession of faith; and we do so, even though their inward lives are further removed from the faith than are those of little children. If this is so, how much more should children be said to have faith when they are solemnly baptized. This is so because they are not opposed to the faith, and they are given in baptism that first and most effectual source of faith.

We can summarize St. Augustine's position in this way: the whole Church is a group of believers, and all of them are honored with this title, both the hypocrites because they make profession, and the true believers because they really believe. Infants also are named believers, because they have made the first step in a spiritual progress to the actual habit of belief. The hypocrite is a believer in the eyes of the world; the true believer is a believer in the sight of God. The infant has made his first step in public profession of the faith in the eyes of the world, and in the development of an actual habit of faith. "This answer," said St. Augustine, "would not please the uninformed or the trouble-maker. It is an answer, however, that will please those who are informed and who do not make trouble. Therefore, I have not given my answer simply in terms of an ancient custom, but I have tried to give you a reasonable answer for a most profitable ceremonial."[2]

Besides the one given by St. Augustine, there is another reason

[2]Migne, S. L. xxxiii. 363.

why questions are asked of infants at their baptism, and why they are answered by the child's sponsors in the child's name. Baptism involves a covenant or contract between God and man; and in this covenant God promises the remission of sins and the gift of his Holy Spirit. God also promises that in the future he will give what other additional help is necessary for the child's attainment of everlasting life. The baptized child receives the grace of kindness of God: that is God's side of the covenant. God receives the promise of obedience: that is the child's side of the covenant. If the child's part in the covenant is faith and newness of life, then the Church must ask of the child a profession of faith and a promise of obedience. Otherwise there is no covenant.

Children may make a covenant with God, even though they cannot do it in their own persons. The children do it through those who undertake the agreement for them. The children's "mother, the Church, provides for them the feet of others to come with, the hearts of others to believe with, the tongues of others to confess with; that as in their sickness they are weighted down by another's sin, so in their cure by another's confession they are made whole."[8] It is true that we do not allow the insane children to make contracts, yet for their own good they are allowed this special consideration and are allowed to make a spiritual contract. It is because of the special benefit they derive from it that the contract of baptism is made for children; and it is because of our tender love for children that the promises made in baptism avail no less than if they had been the children's own.

In the ceremonial of baptism we use the sign of the cross. We sign the child's forehead with a cross as a "token that hereafter he shall not be ashamed to confess the faith of Christ crucified." There are those who condemn the use of the sign of the cross on the ground that it is superstitious. It is not commanded in God's word, they say, and serves no profitable or useful purpose.

[8] Migne, S. L. xxxviii. 950.

Rather, it tends to be magical. Therefore, in our modification and reformation of the liturgy, we should remove it.

Tertullian answers those who do not like any ceremonial usage not found in the Scriptures. "If you should ask that we show you a commandment in Holy Scriptures for the use of the sign of the cross and similar customs, we must answer that there is no such commandment. Our reason for it is the justification of a tradition or custom. This value of the tradition we must observe ourselves in the actual value of the usage, or else learn from someone else who does understand the usage."[4] I know that some people do not like the word tradition, and so we must make clear exactly what we mean by it. By tradition we mean those ordinances established in the early days of Christianity, and continued in use since then. The authority for them is that which Christ left to his Church in all matters which are not contrary to Christianity, and so are indifferent. The Church has the authority to continue such customs and only to alter them where there is just and reasonable cause for doing so. Granted that the sign of the cross is the invention of the Church, that does not mean that we must necessarily remove it. The test is what purpose does it serve? Is it appropriate?

Those who object to the sign of the cross belong to those people who do not like any ceremony to have meaning. Those who make ceremony meaningless ask that people sit when they make their communion simply because the Apostles were at the table when the Eucharist was instituted. But to sit now at a communion is meaningless, and is without profit. Such meaningless ceremonies are mere idle gestures, and are like the acts of half-wits, rather than of those who are in control of life. To make the sitting for the receiving of communion important is to make something of no importance a matter of grave import. What we should consider is whether our ceremony has meaning,

[4] *de Coron. Militis.* c. 4.

and so, in relation to the sign of the cross we should ask whether it is significant and meaningful.

Even our Lord Jesus Christ himself objects when the courteous ceremonies of home life are disregarded. This disregard he does not like, and he did not like it because he preferred the meaningful ceremony which expresses courtesy, and chides those who condemn the courtesy. The woman had washed his feet with her tears, dried them with her hair, and anointed them with ointment. Then, our Lord's host, Simon the Pharisee, condemned her for ceremonial extravagance. Our Lord favors her actions, and chides Simon for his lack of courtesy: "Simon, Seest thou this woman? I entered into thine house, thou gavest me no water for my feet: but she hath washed my feet with tears, and wiped *them* with the hairs of her head. Thou gavest me no kiss: but this woman since the time I came in hath not ceased to kiss my feet. My head with oil thou didst not anoint: but this woman hath anointed my feet with ointment."[5]

The usual ceremonies of our ordinary life are liked or disliked because of what they mean; and this includes the acts we perform without words to show our meaning. In religion too we have silent rites or manual acts, and they have meaning because of what they signify. Their meaning lies in what they indicate, for it is their very nature to point out something. By means of the outer senses they point to something beyond the sensuous. Then if a ceremony points out something that is good, and it is an adequate expression of the good, there is no reason to oppose it. That which is evil should not be expressed, but it is particularly inappropriate to object to ceremonial because it is meaningful.

The ceremony of the sign of the cross admonishes us to glory in the service of Jesus Christ. It is a reminder that we should not hang down our heads in shame because of the reproaches of this wretched world. Reason and religion teach us of what we must be ashamed. However, the things that seem disgraceful,

[5]Lk. 7. 44-46.

although not actually such, tend to bemuse us and make us afraid. In order to keep us from sliding away from our better insights, constant reminders are necessary to keep our attention drawn to the true good. Constant reminders at hand act as a bridle to our offences. This has been the experience of Cato and many good men.[6]

If men of great experience and insight into the limitations of our weak humanity have thought it necessary to have reminders which constantly point to the truth, surely it has been wisdom on the part of the Church of Christ to use the ceremony of the cross in baptism. No Christian should despise the sign of the cross since human nature implores us to furnish aids to the resistance of evil. Such symbols furnish us with a ready assistance and a powerful aid to memory. The sign of the cross reminds us that we should be ashamed of sin.

[6]Sen. Epist. lib. i. Ep. 11.

CHAPTER XXVIII

CONFIRMATION THE COMPLETION OF BAPTISM

IT was the ancient custom of the Church to baptize and then to confirm, for confirmation is the perfection of that new life inaugurated by baptism. The rite of confirmation consists in the imposition of the hands of the bishop upon the head of the child, and of prayers for the illumination of the one confirmed by God's Holy Spirit. The reason why prayers are offered is that through them God's gifts of grace are obtained for the child. When he confirms, the bishop prays for those on whose heads he lays the hands of blessing. God does answer the prayers of persons who make request for those under their authority. God answers the prayers of the natural father in behalf of his children, and he also answers the prayers of the spiritual father for his children. The bishop is a spiritual father, and God hears his request because the bishop stands as a father in relation to his spiritual children.

The rite of confirmation consists in the prayers offered to God by the bishop, and in the laying on of hands. This imposition of hands in blessing is an ancient ceremony for indicating the one whom God is to bless. We are told that when Joseph brought his two sons, Ephraim and Manasseh, for his father's blessing, Israel blessed Joseph's sons, placed his hands on their heads, and prayed to the Almighty and said, "God, before whom my fathers Abraham and Isaac did walk, the God which fed me all my life long unto this day, the Angel which redeemed me from all evil, bless the lads."[1]

The laying on of hands in blessing was used from the time of the Patriarchs to that of Christ. Our Lord used the same custom when he aided those who came to him for help, for he placed

[1] Gen. 48. 15-16.

his hands upon the heads of those who needed his mercy and did great works for the restoration of their bodily health. He also brought about an infusion of heavenly grace in little children whose lives had not yet been so debased as to hinder a gift of God's goodness to them. "'Then were there brought unto him little children, that he should put *his* hands on them, and pray: and the disciples rebuked them. But Jesus said, Suffer little children, and forbid them not, to come unto me: for of such is the kingdom of heaven. And he laid *his* hands on them . . .'"[2]

After our Lord and Saviour Jesus Christ had ascended into heaven, his work was continued by his Apostles. By prayer and the laying on of hands many thousands became partakers of the wonderful gifts of God. Christ had said, "And these signs shall follow them that believe; In my name shall they cast out devils; they shall speak with new tongues; they shall take up serpents; and if they drink any deadly thing, it shall not hurt them; they shall lay their hands on the sick, and they shall recover."[3] At the first, all believers had this power, but all believers did not have the power to communicate this ability to others. Many had the power to instruct, convert, and baptize, but power to give the gift of the miraculous operations of the Holy Ghost came only from the hands of the Apostles.

The miraculous graces of the spirit continued even after the Apostles' time. Some cast out devils; some spoke with tongues; and others restored people to health by the imposition of their hands. The Bishops, as the successors of the Apostles, for a time had this power, and could make others capable of performing the same miraculous works of grace. This continued as long as it pleased God for the successors of the Apostles to have this power. St. Augustine tells us that such gifts were not allowed to last for always, "for when the Catholic Church was diffused and established through the whole world, those miracles were not

[2]Mt. 19. 13-15.
[3]Mk. 16. 17-18.

permitted to last into our times, lest the mind should always demand visible signs, and the human race should wax cold by the commonness of that the strangeness whereof at first inflamed them."[4]

It was only for a short time that the Bishops had the power through prayer and the laying on of hands of bestowing these many miraculous gifts of the Holy Ghost. However, prayer and the laying on of hands have continued as the means of very special benefits in the confirmation of those who have been baptized. The Fathers of the Church tell us that in confirmation there is a gift of the Holy Ghost, but not that gift which first makes us Christians. The first gift of the Holy Ghost is the work of baptism; but confirmation does assist us in all virtue, and fortifies us against temptation and sin.

Tertullian tells us that when baptism has been administered, "there follows the laying on of hands and the invocation of the Holy Ghost. Then the Holy Ghost most willingly comes from the Father to rest upon the purified and blessed bodies. It is as if the Spirit acknowledged that the waters of baptism had found a proper place."[5] Eusebeus Emisenus tells us, "The Holy Ghost first descends upon the waters of baptism, and through them cleanses the child. Then in confirmation he makes a further gift of grace."[6] The Fathers believed that confirmation was an apostolic ordinance which is always of profit. The Epistle to the Hebrews speaks of "the doctrine of baptisms, and of laying on of hands" as belonging to the principles of the doctrine of Christ.[7] Although confirmation was accompanied by more spectacular manifestations at first, it is always profitable in God's Church.

In the beginning confirmation immediately followed baptism, for they usually went together. But in the West they were sepa-

[4]Migne, S. L. xxxiv. 142.
[5]de Baptis. c. 8.
[6]Ser. de Pentec. p. 77.
[7]Heb. 6. 2.

rated from each other, and confirmation followed baptism after a considerable length of time.   The separation of the two services had several causes.   First of all, the deacon or priest could baptize, but only the bishop could confirm.   This was true even in the time of the Apostles, for after Philip had baptized certain persons in Samaria, Peter and John confirmed them.[8]

St. Jerome tells us that the custom of the churches was for the bishop to go about in the further corners of the diocese and to lay his hands on those who had already been baptized by presbyters and deacons.[9]   St. Cyprian uses the precedent of Peter and John as the ground for the separation of baptism and confirmation.   He tells us that Peter and John supplied by confirmation what was omitted in baptism.   That is the reason, says St. Cyprian, why those who have been baptized are brought to the bishop of the Church to obtain the Holy Ghost through prayer and the laying on of hands.[10]   From these illustrations it is clear that in the time of the Fathers baptism, when administered by deacons and priests, was followed by confirmation at the hands of the bishop.

The second reason for the separation of baptism from confirmation was the decision that members of heretical groups, although baptized and confirmed in the schismatic body, should be confirmed by the Church.   There were several manners of handling the repentent heretic who renounced his error.   Sometimes he was both rebaptized and reconfirmed.   The usual procedure, however, was to accept his baptism, but to reconfirm him. There was more than one interpretation as to the meaning of this confirmation of heretics.   One was that heretical baptism gave the remission of sins, but there was no bestowal of the Holy Spirit by the laying on of hands.   St. Jerome reveals the weakness of this argument.   He holds that baptism involves the gifts of

[8]Acts, 8.   12-17.
[9]Migne, S. L. xxxiii.   164.
[10]Migne, S. L. iii.   1115.

the Holy Ghost. It is the Holy Ghost that remits our sins, and without the Holy Ghost there is no remission of sins. If the Holy Ghost is given in baptism, and heretical baptism is accepted, then the argument that heretics cannot convey the gift of the Holy Ghost is not to be accepted.

The gifts of the Holy Ghost are given in baptism. St. Jerome's argument is that the Holy Ghost is given by the sacrament of baptism, and the imposition of the bishop's hands is not necessary for that.[11] The reason why only the bishop confirms is because the benefits of grace confirmed are greater than those in baptism, and the bishop as a spiritual father has the authority of blessing. Since patriarchal times the blessing has been given by those in authority; and the bishop as spiritual father, by prayer and the laying on of hands, invokes added gifts of the Holy Ghost. We now see why St. Jerome holds the doctrine that confirmation is a sacramental complement, and not a sacrament. It is the blessing that reaffirms baptism. It bestows added gifts of the Holy Ghost. It tends to increase in us the fruits of repentance. Like David, the repentant heretic desires a renewal of God's grace. The appropriateness of confirming the heretic who has returned to the bosom of the Church is that confirmation gives a strength for a renewal of life after failure. However, in the child who has not fallen from God, confirmation also gives strength, but strength for fuller life.

The last reason for separating confirmation from baptism is the fact that baptism usually is given to infants. In infancy it is quite appropriate that the child be admitted into the family of the Church, but in his infancy he cannot undertake the full duties of his membership in Christ's Church. It is at a later time that he becomes a soldier in the army of God and discharges the duties of a Christian man. It is later that he brings forth the fruits of the spirit and performs the works of the Holy Ghost. For that reason, it is well that confirmation be delayed. In preparation

[11]Migne, S. L. xxiii. 165.

for confirmation, the child is trained in the principles of true religion before malice and corruption deprave his mind. At confirmation the bishop, to whom all of God's family is entrusted, can examine the children. This not only benefits the child, but allows the bishop to see for his own comfort the earliest beginning of true godliness in the tender years of children. Then the reverend father in God exhorts and encourages the children of the Church as his spiritual charges. Then he lays his hands upon them, prays for them, and blesses them. Anyone who accepts the truth of religion can hardly deny that the blessing of patriarchs, priests, apostles, and bishops cannot be without fruit in the lives of those upon whose heads they place their hands.

CHAPTER XXIX

THE SACRAMENT OF THE EUCHARIST

IT is by baptism that we come to a newness of life; but it is by the Eucharist that we continue our new life. Only after baptism is the Eucharist necessary, because no dead thing is capable of nourishment, and before baptism we are dead in trespasses and sins. Life is needful for growth, and so nourishment is necessary after the restoration of life. Possibly the grace given in baptism would insure our eternal life, if it were not for the sins we commit after receiving it. If our new life needed no restoration, then our souls would not require the Eucharist; but in these days of warfare on earth we do sin, and unless restored by nourishment, our bodies decay and our souls fail. As we must have physical food for our natural bodies, so we must have spiritual food for our souls. That is the reason why our Lord and Saviour says, "Except ye eat the flesh of the Son of man, and drink his blood, ye have no life in you. Whoso eateth my flesh, and drinketh my blood, hath eternal life; and I will raise him up at the last day."[1]

Life is the true end for us, and baptism lays the foundation for our new life in Christ. But the new life requires nourishment, and the food of that new life is the continued abiding in the Son of man, who came to give us life, and that more abundantly. Those of us who would live the life of God must eat the flesh and drink the blood of the Son of man, because without him we cannot have life. In infancy we are incorporated into Christ by baptism. We do not know that we have received the grace of his Holy Spirit, but this is indeed the gift of God bestowed by him on us. In adult life we receive Christ by degrees, and are incorporated into him more and more. This process of increasing

[1] Jn. 6. 53, 54.

in holiness and virtue we know and can judge. We understand the strength of our life, and realize that his flesh is our meat and his blood is our drink. It is no surmise of the imagination that through faith we really do taste eternal life when we sacramentally eat the body and drink the blood of our Lord in the Eucharist.

Despite the many diverse conceptions as to the nature of the Eucharist, it seems impossible to deny that its purpose is our real participation in Christ. Therefore, the endless discussions about it have little meaning if the true end of this sacrament is kept in view. What is really significant is that we are actually incorporated into Christ through it. Much of the controversy rages about the question whether our Lord's body and blood are externally located in the very elements themselves. This is a very secondary matter compared with the recognition of the fact that we are incorporated into Christ by the grace given to us through the Eucharist.

I could wish that men would give themselves to a silent meditation as to what we received by the sacraments and would dispute less as to how we receive it. If this advice seems stupid and dull, let us examine the evidence and learn whether our Lord's Apostles did not do the same thing. They were often very inquisitive, and in some matters of even less importance than the Eucharist they asked our Lord questions. It is a very interesting fact that although he said so little about the high mystery of the Eucharist, the Apostles received this gift with gladness, and asked no questions about it. When we know how we act when we really want things very much, we can understand why the disciples asked no questions. Intricate speculations quench the joy and delight of receiving the thing we deeply desire, and so, if we really enjoy a thing very much, we are not interested in anything else, and tend to cast aside merely intellectual pursuits because they distract from our happiness. The disciples were not interested in elaborate conceptions, and when the gift of Christ was given them, they did not speculate and form opinions about God's gifts, but they tasted and found that God was good.

The fruit of the Eucharist is the participation in the body and the blood of Christ; and this the disciples understood and appreciated. When Christ says "this is my body", and "this is my blood", these are words not so much of theological explanation as of promise: he promises us that we are to participate in his life. Through his omnipotent power he creates his body and blood in us. Whether there is a change in the elements themselves does not greatly concern us, as long as we admit that through the sacrament we are incorporated into Christ. As Bellarmine says about the sacraments in general, "For faith it is sufficient that it be proved from faith and the Scriptures that the sacraments are the cause of grace. How it happens it is very difficult to understand, and it never can be explained. That is not to be wondered at, for if God does something in the natural world, although we see it we are not able to explain it. How much more difficult it is to make clear supernatural things to the reason. The schoolmen, when they discuss these matters, do something that is not without value. They are demonstrating that matters of faith can be defended in various ways. They teach us what the faith says, and what may probably be said about it. Their opinions, however, do not pertain to the faith itself."[2]

In the matter of the Eucharist, I accept that in which all schools agree; and all agree that through this sacrament we participate in Christ. Since it is agreed that we really do participate in Christ through the Eucharist, this is our basic conception of its meaning. In this sacrament Christ imparts himself, and he imparts himself in his entire person, and he imparts himself as the mystical fountain of life and head of every soul who receives him.

[2]Opera, iii. 119, 120.

In the Eucharist, each member is united to Christ as a mystical member of our Lord's body; and that is the first point of agreement. The second point of agreement is that when we participate in Christ through the Eucharist, he gives his Holy Spirit to each of us who receives the sacrament, and that the Spirit sanctifies each of us as it does Christ in whom we are incorporated. In the third place, it is agreed that through the Eucharist we receive the virtue of his sanctified body and blood; and in the fourth place, it is agreed that through the sacrament there is a real transmutation of our bodies and souls from sin to righteousness and from death and corruption to immortality and life. In the fifth place, it is agreed that the sacramental elements are but earthly things, and would seem unlikely instruments to do such marvelous things for man. Our only course of action, therefore, is to rely upon the strength of God's glorious power, for he is willing and able to do the things which through the grace he gives us we can do.

Blessed and praised forever be his name who perceives of what heavy and senseless stuff we are made, and has instituted and in his Church prepared a spiritual Eucharist for us. Through it the Christ of God is truly united to us and we to him. As the arm is united to the shoulder, so we are united to Christ; and he dwells in us just as really as the elements of bread do. If we are persuaded of this truth, when we receive these dreadful mysteries and receive them truly, we receive comfort through them. For this reason, we speak of "the most comfortable Sacrament of the Body and Blood of Christ." If we receive the sacrament unworthily, then, as the Apostle says, we do it to our damnation. Hence, when we put forth our hands and receive this blessed sacrament, we are charged to examine and try our heart to see if we are prepared to receive the elements worthily. In the *Invitation* we are told, "Ye who do truly and earnestly repent you of your sins, and are in love and charity with your neighbors, and intend to lead a new life, following the commandments of God, and walking from henceforth in his holy ways; Draw near with faith, and take his holy Sacrament to your comfort; and make your humble confession to Almighty God, devoutly kneeling."

In one of the *Exhortations* we are told, ". . . as the benefit is great, if with a true penitent heart and lively faith we receive the holy Sacrament; so is the danger great, when we receive the same unworthily." This leads to the injunction, "Judge therefore yourselves, brethren, that ye be not judged of the Lord; repent you truly for your sins past; have a lively and stedfast faith in Christ our Saviour; amend your lives, and be in perfect charity with all men; so shall ye be meet partakers of those holy mysteries." Only then can we approach the table of the Lord, but if we find ourselves among those who have "offended, either by will, word, or deed," then we must "confess to Almighty God, with full purpose of amendment of life." Only as we worthily receive are we truly united to Christ.

If we receive as we ought, the wine is not like the water of Marah, a bitter cup; but it is like the cup of blessing for us. If we receive aright, the bread is not a manna steeped in gall, but it is like the true manna in the wilderness. If we receive worthily, there is a taste of Christ Jesus in our hearts as we eat of the spiritual manna. If we receive worthily, the wine of the cup is the blood of the lamb to bathe our souls. Beloved of our Lord and Saviour, Jesus Christ, if ye only taste the sweetness of our Lord, ye will receive the King of glory within your souls.

CHAPTER XXX

The Reception of the Eucharist

W E are exhorted to examine ourselves before we eat the bread and drink the cup of the Eucharist; and to examine ourselves is our bounden duty. It is another question, however, whether we should require every man to give an account of himself before he receives the Eucharist. It is sometimes argued that the Apostles required such an examination; but there is no record that they did so. Those who make such a demand use the precedent of preparation for the Old Testament Passover; and they use as their proof the words of the Lord God of the Levites, "So kill the passover, and sanctify yourselves, and prepare your brethren, that *they* may do according to the word of the Lord . . ."[1] But this passage only commands that the people be prepared to participate in the service in a seemly manner. There is no indication that there was an examination of the people as to their personal fitness to eat the Passover.

There is a demand that everyone receiving the Eucharist should behave himself strictly in accordance with the demands of the Gospel, and that all persons with any strange doctrines should be kept from the House of God. However, it is difficult to know who are those who are perfectly obedient to the Gospel, because the visible Church of Christ includes many who are not members of the Kingdom of God. These we must admit, therefore, to the Eucharist unless they are notorious evil-doers.

When we speak of the Church, we mean that society of men who profess the true religion of Jesus Christ, and are by that fact separated from those who do not accept that religion. From the very foundation of the world, there have been three sorts of

[1] 2 Chr. 35. 6.

religion: paganism, Judaism, and Christianity. Paganism includes all those who live in blindness and are guided only by our
corrupt and depraved human nature. Judaism follows the Law,
and looks for the one whom God was to send as the Messiah.
However, the Messiah did come, and so Christianity obeys the
Gospel of Jesus Christ, and acknowledges him to be the Messiah
God promised the Jews.

In any definition of a real thing we pass over those characteristics which are incidental and unessential; and we concentrate on
the essential properties of the thing defined. So we do not stress
those characteristics which make the object better or worse. For
example, if we are defining *man*, we leave out of account these
qualities which make one man better than another, and concentrate on the essential characteristics which make man as man
different from all other creatures. The same thing is true of our
definition of the Church. When we define it, we indicate those
characteristics which make it a community of believers in Christ's
religion, and we indicate those characteristics which separate
them from those who follow any other religion. As religion
is partly a matter of thought and partly a matter of action, we
define the Church by those credal differences and those actions
which distinguish it from other religions. However, from both
points of view, that which separates our religion from all other
religions is Jesus Christ, for no other religion except that of the
Church both believes and worships him. The Apostles always
distinguished the Church from infidels and Jews by the fact that
the Church believes and worships Jesus Christ.[2]

Now, if we wish, we can add to this characterization of the
Church certain variable characteristics or accidents. These do
not form part of the definition of the Church, but they do indicate
the more excellent state that the Church may have in thought
and in deed. There are theologians who so define the Church
that they demand a kind of perfection of her which is a product

[2]Rom. 10. 13.

merely of their own imagination. Others indicate the nature of the Church's possible perfection, but they do not thereby indicate her essential properties. Of course, imperfections do blemish the unity of the Church of Christ, but even the strifes and contentions, even the schisms and factions, only make the body of the Church sick, but do not destroy it. That which makes the Church the Church is first the outward profession of the Lord Jesus Christ as the blessed Saviour of mankind, and second, the reverence and use of the sacraments as the seals of eternal life.

The visible Church of God is like the Ark of Noah, for in it all who are saved are to be found. Yet there is a difference between the Ark and the Church, for all those in the Ark were saved from death in the flood, but all those in the Church will not inherit eternal life. That is because profession of belief in Jesus Christ is not enough to make us members of the kingdom of God, since there are many things which exclude us from the kingdom of God, and yet do not separate us from the Church.

It is true that throughout all the ages there have been heretics, and they have been repudiated as branches cut off the vine. Yet they are not completely cut off, but only in so far as their heresies extend. Heresy and many other offences do separate us from God, but they do not completely separate us from the Church of God. The Church is the pillar and foundation of truth, and nowhere else is this truth known and professed except in it. Nevertheless, there are many who profess this truth, and yet through their faults and errors are separated from the fountain of eternal happiness. Therefore, the Church of God may have two sorts of members who are not of the kingdom of God. The first are those who are not his own, and yet we count them as his because they outwardly conform but are inwardly evil. Second, there are those who are wicked enough that we can see that God abhors them. That is the meaning of those parables of the tares and the drawnet. The tares were allowed to remain in the field because their removal would have destroyed the good grain. Our Lord knew that the visible Church would be a mixture of vice with virtue, light with darkness, truth with error. Sometimes this mixture of good and evil is apparent; at other times it is so cunningly devised that we cannot see it.

The thing, however, which cuts off and completely separates members from the visible Church of Christ is outright apostasy. It is the direct denial and the utter rejection of Christianity in its essential difference from infidelity. A heretic is cut off from the Church of Christ in regard to those points of doctrine in which he is in error; a schismatic is cut off from the Church of Christ through his quarrels with his brethren; a loose and licentious person is cut off from the Church of Christ through his offences and crimes. The heretic is cut off from the Church through the unsoundness of his doctrine; the schismatic is cut off from the Church through his disruption of her unity; the licentious man is cut off from the Church through his unrighteousness. Yet none of these is completely separated from the Church, for they have not completely forsaken her. Many still build on the foundations of the Church although they have destroyed much of the superstructure.

God does not require of us to pry into men's consciences, since fraud and deceit only hurt those who deceive. God knows men as they are, but we must take men as they seem to be. If any man is not openly opposed to Christ, we must receive him as one with Christ, even though he is against Christ in the eyes of God. It is different in the case of notorious sinners, for we must exclude them from the reception of the Eucharist. These impenitent ones are different from those who have some unseen error of doctrine or secret fault hidden from our sight. The notorious sinner is different from the man who wishes the sacrament at our hands, and yet may be secretly schismatic or heretical in his heart. It cannot reasonably be held against us, if we admit these to the holy sacraments without prying into their minds to determine the exact nature of their consciences. Curiously to enquire into every man's life is to impose on the Church the task of probing further into men's hearts than any law of God or man requires. There is danger that under the severity of too much inquiry we may repel from the mysteries of heavenly grace those who need the Eucharist and who are capable of receiving it. It is better to show mercy than to be rigorous beyond the requirement of God's compassion. The Gospel of Christ has taught us mercy and compassion. If the Eucharist can strengthen any man, then his weakness should be augmented by power; and so wherever there is any foundation we should build upon it. Even a slender foundation should be perfected, since our Lord came not for the whole but for the sick, and the Eucharist has been left by Christ to his Church as the food of life for the preservation of our strength and the relief of our weakness.

We do need the blessed sacrament as the food to strengthen us at every time when life perplexes us, since it is given to us as the food and drink of eternal life. Our general consolation, both in life and death, is the resurrection from death and the life everlasting; and this life and this resurrection of our Lord Jesus Christ is for all men, and was made possible once and for all by his sacrifice for us. However, we only become partakers of his life and his death by our individual communion with Christ; and the sacrament of the Eucharist is the principal means of strengthening the bond between us and him. As St. Ignatius tells us, the Eucharist is "a medicine which procures immortality and prevents death."[3] Irenaeus says that it is the nourishment of our bodies to eternal life.[4] When minds are troubled and grieved, the conditions of all men's lives are much alike. Then it is the charitable order of the Church in which we live to grant the reasonable petitions of those in distress, and we administer the blessed sacrament to those whose desires are

[3] Migne, S. G. vii. 1027.
[4] Migne, S. G. iv. 923.

kindled for it. The Church in her compassion grants this means of grace to all who in any sense conform to her; and both in life and in death she administers every help which Christian mercy and compassion can afford.

DATE DUE